THE
FIRE
IS COMING

W Zephania

WESTBOW
PRESS®
A DIVISION OF THOMAS NELSON
& ZONDERVAN

WestBow Press books may be ordered through booksellers or by contacting:

WestBow Press
A Division of Thomas Nelson & Zondervan
1663 Liberty Drive
Bloomington, IN 47403
www.westbowpress.com
844-714-3454

ISBN: 978-1-6642-2889-4 (sc)
ISBN: 978-1-6642-2888-7 (e)

Print information available on the last page.

WestBow Press rev. date: 3/31/2021

This book is dedicated to my mother, who went to be with the Lord Jesus on May 28ᵗʰ 2020 after a struggle with Dementia and Covid 19. She passed away with her hand in my sister's and I am so grateful to God that she was there with her and she was not alone. Thanks mom, for being such a hardworking inspiration to us all and for all you did for us. Until we meet again in glory be blessed.

Thanks to all the doctors, nurses, carers and family members, who gave such loving care to my mom, God bless you one and all.

BOOK REVIEWS

This is my latest book. I want to show you how the street work has developed by giving you an update because much has happened since 2015 when I wrote my first book following twenty years of serving on the city streets. God is always working on the city streets and it is a privilege to gather in the harvest with the Holy Spirit as we learn to respond to His impulses together. I hope you will enjoy the format of the book as it is peppered with testimonies and real- life stories as well as prophetic insights from the Word of God.

INTRODUCTION

This book looks at some bible principals and people transformed by the limitless power of the Living God from the city streets. Behind every person in the Bible there is a revelation or unveiling waiting to be discovered like some long- lost treasure of immeasurable wealth and beauty. In this book you will discover how and why God uses ordinary broken people to communicate with us and get our attention. You will discover people on a journey feeling lost, broken, hopeless, being transformed by God's extravagant grace and love for them, even in the midst of incredibly difficult circumstances and situations.

God's greatest passion is for a deep, meaningful and intimate relationship with mankind, created in His image and likeness. He has designed us to know and enjoy Him forever. Come with me on a journey of questioning and discovery, which will ultimately lead us into deeper realms of God as we encounter Him and hear from many ordinary people transformed through living encounters with Him.

Any names in this book are only given by permission. Real names have always been shared with permission of all individuals involved in sharing their personal stories. It is my privilege to work alongside most of the people mentioned in this book and to give them an opportunity to share their stories with anyone interested in listening. I thank them all for their willingness to share because I know they are doing it to bless and encourage every reader of this book.

To get the most out of this book Scripture references are given so please use them and meditate on the true words of God and you will find life and radiant health for your whole body, mind and spirit. Proverbs 4: 20-23 TPT.

POEM

Where do they go and who do they turn to?

O God if Your there, help me to find You. I Know I'm lost but I don't know how to find You. Please send somebody to help me to find You, one of Your children God.

Will you help them or will you just watch them from a distance and remain silent? They are God's hidden treasure in a field needing to be uncovered. He has given everything He ever had to buy the field to save them. He is the jewel merchant in search of very precious, rare and exquisite pearls, who gives up all He has in exchange for them. He has sold all He possessed and given up all He had just so He could have His treasure. He needs you and I to go and tell them they are His treasure. We are the spark that lights the fire within their hearts, the passionate fire of the Father's love for them. One treasure must go to another, yet to be uncovered.

He wants to share the joys of bringing them home with us, rather than doing it all alone because they are brothers and sisters. Put your hand in the hand of the Holy Spirit and go out together looking for them and be amazed and surprised by those you meet. There they in the market place, on the streets of our cities, usually standing all alone and looking for salvation and forgiveness but not knowing how. O God if Your there, please help me to find You. Matthew 13: 44-46 TPT.

THE VISION

There was once a man who climbed a mountain. At the top of the mountain, he paused to take in the views, rest and pray and as he prayed, he had a vision. In the vision, he saw a great ocean stretching from one horizon to another. The seas began to churn as a mighty storm arose and a great sea beast rose out of the waters with many horns on its head. The beast was terrifying, dreadful and strong. It devoured and crushed its victims with huge iron teeth and trampled their remains beneath its feet. As the man looked at the beast's horns, suddenly another small horn appeared among them. Three of the other horns were torn out by the roots to make room for it. The small horn had eyes like human eyes and a mouth that boasted arrogantly. Suddenly as the man watched, thrones were put in place and the Ancient of Days sat down on His throne ready to judge. His clothing was as white as snow and His hair like purest wool. He sat on a fiery throne with wheels of blazing fire and a river of fire was flowing out from His presence. Millions of angels ministered to Him, many millions stood to attend Him. Then the court began its session and the books were opened. The little horn continued its boastful speech as the man watched until the beast was killed and its body destroyed by fire. The man's vision continued and he saw someone like a Son of Man coming with the clouds of heaven. He approached the Ancient of Days and was led into His presence. He was given authority, honour and sovereignty over all the nations of the world, so that people of every race, nation and language would obey Him. His rule is eternal, it will never end. His Kingdom will never be destroyed.

The man who had the vision was Daniel and his vision is about to be fulfilled.

1

THE FIRE IS COMING

S ome months past now, I had the most powerful dream I have
ever had, so powerful I awoke in the middle of it sobbing into
my pillow. In the dream I was looking up into the night sky and it
suddenly became red with fire from one end to the other. A man
suddenly appeared in the dream whom I recognised as a minister in
Inverness and we hugged one another with joy as a result of the fire.
This man was saved in Inverness just before me and his testimony was
very powerful and influential at the time of his salvation among the
youth in Inverness. I then heard the Holy Spirit saying three times that
the fire is coming, the fire is coming, the fire is coming! At this point I
woke up and my pillow was wet with tears because I had been weeping
into it throughout the dream.

God is about to send such a fire into this nation that it will never
be the same again. That fire will unite believers from all denominations
to bring in the greatest revival harvest the world has ever seen. We are
about to be baptised in the Holy Spirit and fire. God is purifying us to
be ready to carry the fire to the nations and release signs, wonders and
miracles like never before. We have tasted little glimmers of fire up to
now but nothing like what I saw in my dream and it is coming. Fire is

used by God to purify His people and consecrate us to Him for good works which glorify His Name. The fire is coming.

The fire is part of the glory of God. John said he had seen His glory. John 1: 14. His glory is who He is as well as what he has said and done. His glory will be in what He has still to do now and in the age to come. Before creation existed, there was glory and it was a shared glory between the Trinity of God. The new creation will also demonstrate the glory of God. What exactly is glory? Three of Jesus' disciples saw the glory of Jesus, Moses and Elijah on a mountain as Jesus became glorified right in front of them. Luke 9: 28-36. There is a glory realm and these three disciples found themselves in it on a mountain top. Once in it they were told to listen to Him. The glory realm is firstly the place of revelation from God to man. The gospel message or Good News reveals the glory of Christ to sinful men that we might be saved. In the gospel, Jesus is revealed as Lord and when we confess Him as Lord, we are saved. Paul describes the gospel as a light shining in our hearts revealing the glory of God to us. 2 Corinthians 4: 4-6. The glory realm is a holy realm.

The blood of Jesus, the Lamb of God gives us access to the glory realm, to the face of Jesus and His eyes of burning fire. Revelation 1: 10-20. As John worshiped in the Spirit, he entered into the glory realm and so must we. John fell at His feet as though dead until Jesus laid His right hand upon him, it can be a fearful place the glory realm. I've been there once before and could only lie face down with my eyes tightly shut for the fear of God had come upon me and an acute awareness of my sinfulness in His presence. It is something unforgettable that marks us forever. It is a supernatural realm which makes the human body feel uncomfortable as we feel the sinfulness of sin. It is a place to repent and receive God's forgiveness and cleansing deeply. We were created to live in the glory realm and the blood of Jesus has made this possible once again. His blood speaks to God in heaven for us before the mercy seat and opens the way for us to enter in. Hebrews 10.

The glory realm awaits as the place of revelation, fire, cleansing and purification for the purposes of God but there is more. In Isaiah 6: 1-13 the prophet has entered the glory realm where he receives his calling and his anointing. We receive our call to make Christ known through His Good News in the glory realm as His light shines into our hearts. 2 Cor 4: 4-6. When we simply share God's Good News with others, we are revealing truth from the glory realm, revealing Christ who is the Way, the Truth and the Life. When Stephen shared God's truth with his executioners his face shone like the face of an angel. Acts 6: 15. It is the place of revelation, fire, cleansing, calling and intimacy as Isaiah, Moses and Joshua were to discover. Every time we share truth from God's glory realm here on earth, we are entering the glory realm.

In Exodus 33: 7- 34: 8 we see Moses entering into God's glory realm where he speaks to God face to face and discovers intimacy with God. Like Joshua we want to remain there for more of God. Even though Moses was permitted to speak to God face to face, he was not allowed to see His face as Christ had yet to be revealed to mankind. We only see the glory of God in the face of Jesus Christ. John saw this glory as he recognised the Word had become human flesh and was living among us for a season of time. So, the glory realm is the place of revelation, fire, cleansing, calling and intimacy with God face to face. It is the place where our hearts can become entwined to God's and one with His passions and purposes. In the glory realm, God writes His new name upon us, Revelation 2: 17; 26; 3: 4-5; 10-12; 3: 14-22. There is a door standing open in the heavenly glory realm where we are invited to come up and in to be shown what must happen after this. Revelation 4: 1. The fire is coming and we must be fire carriers from the glory realm.

When we sit enthroned under the shadow of Shaddai, we are hidden in the strength of God Most High. Psalm 91: 1 TPT.

I brought glory to You here on earth by finishing the work You gave Me to do. John 17: 4.

And we confidently and joyfully look forwards to sharing in God's glory. Romans 5: 2.

There is a false teaching around which fails to emphasise that we are called to be finishers of the faith to which we were called and we must persevere to the end in order to continue to be saved because our great salvation is past, present and future. Difficult times lie ahead for us all, times the Bible describes as troubled times. It is wishful thinking to imagine we will all escape these times so we must allow God to prepare and equip us for them. In Ephesians Paul tells us God is about to do things way beyond our imaginations, dreams and requests because He has big plans and purposes to release as yet into this world through His Church. Ephesians 3: 14-21. The fire is coming through ordinary believers like us and it will burn brightly for all to see and be purified and set apart for glory. If we want to be a part of this great end times harvest from the nations we need to daily walk with God and serve Him faithfully right up to the end. I encourage you to align your life again into the plans and purposes of God through repentance and turning back to Him. He is so good, so ready to forgive, so full of unfailing love towards you. Psalm 86: 5.

Proverbs is the only book in the Bible that claims to be the key to unlock the treasures of true knowledge, giving us access to kingdom revelations, wisdom, insight and understanding. Proverbs 1: 1-2 TPT. With these keys we can open doors to right choices, wise relationships, true knowledge, design and destiny, deeper meanings and brilliant strategies for leadership. I'm sure, like me, you could do with many of these qualities in your personal walk with God. The Church and the world are waiting to see God's true children rise up and use these keys to unlock the great harvest promised before Christ's return. A key has little value unless taken and used for the specific purpose for which it was designed. There are many different treasures of divine knowledge yet to be accessed by the children of God using God's proverbial keys.

The keys are also given to open our understanding of the many parables, poetic riddles and enigmas in the Bible, including the parables taught by Jesus. To be able to use our keys we must be living in the fear of the Lord or walking in submission, awe, worship and reverence for God. We pass from darkness to wisdom's light by our fear of the Lord. God chooses to reveal Himself as both a Father and a Mother in Proverbs. Proverbs 1: 8. TPT. He has the heart of both for us, His beloved children. He wants us to enjoy success, grace-filled thoughts, humble decision making. Wisdom is singing a song in Proverbs but not necessarily in the halls of the higher learning institutions of this world. She chooses to sing in the hustle and bustle of everyday life where God wants to be involved with us. We can share even the most mundane with Him so that we experience abundant life or life in all its fullness. John 10: 10. He wants to give us more than we are expecting until we are overflowing. It is only as we learn to overflow, that we give out to others in need from our abundance. Revelation from God's words makes our hearts wise, creates peace within, releases us from fear and gives us confidence and courage in the storms of life. Our hearts were created for His wisdom and our spirits created to be expanded through discernment. Our souls created to experience pleasure through God's revelations. Proverbs 2: 1-15.

Would you like a long and satisfying life and a full, rewarding life? Cultivate a humble, teachable heart that longs to be obedient and God's promise of life will be yours. God wants us to live well by living with integrity and loyalty to both God and men. Proverbs 3: 1-4. We are living in a world where people love to share their opinions on everything under the sun. It is okay to have opinions but never to rely upon them because they may be fallible if not built on a firm foundation. There are opinions on everything from conspiracies to the rapture but are they full of God's wisdom, insight and understanding? Perhaps not! There are certain things God deliberately hides from us for our own good, we must accept that our human knowledge is limited so we trust in Him completely. He promises to guide us by His Spirit in every decision we need to make. Proverbs 3: 5-6; Isaiah 55: 8-9; Deuteronomy 29: 29.

In 1 Corinthians 2: 1-16, Paul is speaking about the wisdom of God revealing His mysteries. He is speaking about Jesus Christ, the One crucified for us. He is speaking about the mystery of His secret plan, previously hidden, now revealed in the birth, death and resurrection of His Son. Even though God's plan was made for our ultimate glory before the world began, it has only been revealed since Christ's coming and the preaching of the Good News subsequent to His ascension. It is perhaps God's greatest secret now revealed to us by the Holy Spirit so that we can know the wonderful things God has freely given us. We can only understand the glory of these things because we as believers have the mind of Christ. As we meditate on the holy Scriptures filled by the Spirit with the mind of Christ, we can use the keys to open up the revelations God has given to us. We are to do this daily to build up our faith and strengthen and encourage one another in the Body of Christ. God will also drop prophetic insights into our spirits for people he wants us to speak to during the day, so that they too can become believers when they experience the love and power of God. He wants to prepare and equip us for every situation planned for us in the days to come by meeting with us as we spend quality time with Him. We met a man recently in Argyle Street who initially seemed quite aggressive but as we listened to him God began to give us insights which we shared and he changed immediately. As we prayed these prophetic insights into his heart he broke down and wept as he realised God knew him, loved him and was for him, not against him. It was incredible to witness the Holy Spirit at work partnering with us, such a privilege to help this man of God in the making. We owe it to hurting people to share true revelation of God and lead them into His loving arms for salvation. Surely this is one of the main reasons God has given the Holy Spirit to come and live inside of us so that we will be moved by His impulsiveness and take a risk to bless others from His abundance. Romans 8: 14 TPT. The mature children of God are those and only those, who are moved by the impulses of the Holy Spirit. An impulse is a feeling, an emotion and a sensing that is supernaturally given by God to us into our spirits by the Holy Spirit to help others. All it requires on our part is a listening ear, patience and faith to step out and give it at the right time, God will do the rest.

God also uses our God given common sense, which He develops in us as we get to know Him and His ways through obedience to His word. Common sense is no less spiritual than any other sense. Using a mixture of common sense and Spirit given sense is a good and powerful combination. Proverbs is a book full of both Spirit sense and common sense and a chapter a day throughout the month is a great habit to implement. There is nothing like the word of God and the Spirit to stimulate the mind of Christ in us.

In 2 Samuel 22: 31 we read that God's way is perfect and all of His promises prove true. Abram was looking for adventure when he found God. God invites him into an adventure when He invites him to leave and go. Are you willing to go on an adventure with God because that is exactly what He is offering you right now? God's call is the same for us all and He promises blessing, multiplication and joyfulness if we say yes to Him. God's promises to Abram are outrageous because his wife is barren and cannot have children but God is looking beyond that to something bigger and greater, you and me. All the families on earth will be blessed through you Abram. He is called but he must respond by faith because God's promises are activated by faith and faith demonstrated by obedience. Every day for Abram would be a faith day one day at a time as he trusted God to show him where to go that day. We have exactly the same calling of faith as our pioneer Abram. He lived a nomadic wandering lifestyle with loose connections to this world but deep connections to the heavenly world. He was a citizen of heaven living on earth.

When Abram was 99, El- Shaddai or God the Almighty again appears to him and invites him into an even deeper covenant relationship with Him. Age is no barrier to God unless we allow it to be so. God changes his name to father of many or Abraham promising him that his seed descendants would become kings and nations, kings like David and nations like Israel. Abram who cannot father any becomes Abraham the father of many! God promises him the entire land of Canaan as his inheritance to him and his seed forever as an eternal promise and this is why Israel thrives today and will do so forever. God marks Abraham to set him apart for Himself by circumcision and He does so today by the mark of the Holy Spirit in all faith filled believers. We are spiritually circumcised today by the complete cutting away of our old sinful natures.

In Proverbs 8 and 9 we see lady Wisdom shouting and crying out in the public streets for people passing by to come and listen. She is concerned about them because they are lost without God and His wisdom. She wants them to receive knowledge, counsel and correction. She is God's great evangelist calling the people to fear God because there is a bitter fruit to living our own way and not God's. Her message is very simple, fear the Lord and hate all evil. She is calling us all into the faith way, Abram's way which is God's way.

Many of us need to press on, forget the past and focus on finishing our race to receive our prize. We need to develop spiritual maturity and move on from the things of the past not allowing them to determine our future. As far as the past is concerned, we need to crucify our hurts, disappointments, fears and offences. We need to put them to death so that we can concentrate on the future and finish our race. We are called to live as citizens of heaven who are not enemies of the cross of Christ. How do we become friends to the cross? We must practice aligning our thinking and behaviour to heavenly perspective, heavenly goals, heavenly expectations. This is what Abram did when he chose God's way of faith and obedience. This is lady Wisdom's call to all of us children of God Most High, it is the call of the way of the cross. The world wants nothing to do with the way of the cross and the cross wants nothing to do with the way of the world apart from saving it. John 3: 16-17.

In the days to come many will compromise and choose to live as enemies of the way of the cross! Do not be one of them. Christ has given us a new name just as He gave Abram a new name. We are heirs of the same promises and the same covenant spiritually in Christ. We are called to live as friends of the cross, with heavenly perspective, goals and expectations. God is baptizing us in the Holy Spirit and fire and the fire is purifying us to save the world and become a part of God's solution through good, righteous behaviour and relationships. It will be costly for we are citizens of heaven on the way of the cross. God's way is higher and His thoughts higher, it is His way and we must never compromise. It is the power of God for the salvation of all who will believe. Romans 1: 16-17.

The way of the cross is God's perfect way purchased for man's freedom with His own sinless, spotless blood, it cost God and it will cost us so we must never compromise and endure to the end to be saved. Philippians 3: 12-21. By living in the power and shadow of the cross in these last days we can follow Jesus on His narrow way. If we live this way we will not be shaken or surprised by suffering and persecution because we are friends of the cross. Our freedoms to speak out and live out what we believe are under scrutiny like never before as society attempts to mould all into its Godless, hellish shape. We must not compromise and continue to speak up for grace, justice, truth and the way of the cross. We must do so like Jesus who is full of grace and truth remembering that grace always comes before truth. When we are full of God's grace or love in action, those we are dealing with are much more open to receive His truth. John 1: 14. This is the way of the cross it is the way of grace and truth. As you read through this book ask God to cleanse and purify your heart and life with His holy fire from heaven so that you will carry the fire with all wisdom and touch many on your adventure of faith and obedience with God.

In Jeremiah 20: 9 the prophet declares that God's Word was like a fire shut up in His bones which he had to let out as it was far too hot to handle. We are about to experience the same intensity of fire in our witness to the world. This kind of fire will change us forever because we will become hot rather than cold or lukewarm and that changes everything. When the first believers in Acts received the fire, they became fearless and totally unstoppable. The fire that is coming will come in three waves each with a greater intensity and those receiving it will never be the same again. Believers who had been in hiding behind closed doors suddenly became fearless witnesses travelling everywhere telling all the Good News and performing wonders and miracles. The fire within had burnt up all their fears and self- consciousness and replaced it with a burning passionate fire to speak about the wonders of Jesus Christ. Would you like this fire because once it comes there's no going back into hiding?

Even the threats of the authorities could not douse their fire which had to manifest to the glory of God. To become channels of this kind of fire we must first become flammable and willing to burn from the inside out so that we are purified and deeply cleansed by God's refining fire. Some fires have the capacity to burn away bush and clear space for new growth and freshness which sprouts very quickly afterwards. The old is gone and new fresh growth appears with the capacity to nourish and sustain life in different forms. When Moses was drawn to the burning bush, he noticed that although on fire it was not consumed rather it glowed with an intensity of life he had never seen before.

This is a picture of the life of a believer filled with God's passionate fire. Elijah called for fire from heaven which when it came licked up everything in its path that stood in the way of the people knowing God because they had been worshiping idols. The idols were exposed when they saw the true and living God at work and the God of Elijah was to be feared above all others. 1 Kings 18: 20-40.

Fire is one of God's special elements which He uses to further His purposes. The throne of God's government sits on flaming wheels and God sits on a fiery throne with wheels of blazing fire. Daniel 7: 9. A river of fire was pouring out, flowing from His presence. Wherever we have His presence, we also have His fire. Ezekiel 1: 26-28 and 10: 6-8. Psalm 97: 3. In Hebrews we are warned that God is shaking the heavens and the earth, so that only the unshakable will remain. The Kingdom of God is unshakable and God is about to give it to His Son and His people. Psalm 2. Hebrews 12: 25-29. We need to be thankful and worship God with holy fear and awe for all He is about to do with fire. He is a devouring fire and a creating fire as one fire devours the temporal and unclean while another births the permanent and holy. 1 Corinthians 3: 12-14. All around God, burns a blazing glory fire ready to consume all His foes and birth His everlasting Kingdom. Malachi 3: 2 and 4: 1-3 tells us God is a refining fire only leaving behind that which has lasting and eternal value. In Revelation 20: 7-10 we see that fire has the last word as God again unleashes fire from heaven to devour Satan and his armies surrounding His people and His holy city.

God has promised never again to destroy the earth by a flood but not by fire. Genesis 9: 12-17 and 2 Peter 3: 1-13. It seems there is a special kind of fire reserved for the day of judgement that will consume fire itself, which is one of the elements. The very heavens will be set on fire and the elements will melt away in the flames. This fire is a devouring and a creative fire where everything is made new. Revelation 21: 1-27. On that first day when God raised Jesus from the dead, God began a new creation of man in His image and likeness. Jesus is the firstborn of a new creation in reverse of the first which ended with men. When we are resurrected, we will follow Him and witness God's whole new heaven and earth creation birthed from His resurrection. He makes all things new. This is such an exciting promise for the children of God as our destiny is to rule and reign with Him as joint heirs with Christ and heirs of God.

In 2 Thessalonians 1: 7-10, we read that Jesus is coming back to reign on earth with His mighty angels in flaming fire. Why flaming fire? We are told it is the flaming fire of God's judgement on those who do not know God and have refused to obey Him by believing His Good News. They are people who have rejected God and His message, which is the offer of salvation through the death of His Son on the cross. The punishment for rejecting God and His saving grace is eternal destruction and eternal separation from God and His glorious power. Only those belonging to God the Father and the Lord Jesus Christ will be saved. This is what it means to be truly free, it means to belong to God the Father and Jesus Christ our Lord. John 8: 32. Whom do you belong to? If you give and present yourself just as you are, weak and sinful, to Christ, asking for His forgiveness then He can and will save you. A great exchange occurs at the cross where Jesus takes away our sinfulness and gives us His righteousness by grace or love in action. Then we are saved from the coming wrath and judgement of God against sin because God is holy and just therefore sin must face divine justice. 1 Thessalonians 5: 9-10.

But Christ proved God's passionate love for us by dying in our place while we were still lost and ungodly. Romans 5: 8 TPT. God's love is passionate but so is His justice and both are satisfied at the cross but to reject the cross means there is no way to escape the justice of God. If you give yourself to God today and receive His salvation by calling on His Name you will be saved. Romans 10: 9 and following. Open the door of your heart today and receive Christ Jesus as your Lord and Owner and He will wash away all your sins and make you a new creation, belonging to Him. Only God Himself can give us the right and authority to belong to Him and become a son or daughter. John 1: 12. The blood of Jesus is God's perfect, sinless sacrifice for our sins against Him and other people. Oh, precious is the flow that makes us white as snow, no other fount I know, nothing but the blood of Jesus. 1 Peter 1: 17-20 and 1 Peter 3: 18-22.

Christ's passion is God's passionate way of salvation for all mankind. He alone is the Light of the world. We must come His way and believe in what He has done for us in order to be saved and it is Good News. It is God taking the initiative to save us. It is God's solution to our sin problem. It is the way of the cross. Acts 4: 12. The flaming fire is coming and we need to be saved from it or we are lost. 2 Thessalonians 2: 1-12. God's truth is given to us to be obeyed not rejected. A man of lawlessness is coming who will lead many astray through counterfeit power, signs and miracles, a modern- day false Saviour of the world. This man will further the work of Satan by inciting great rebellion against God and even claiming to be God. His time to be revealed is coming but the Lord Jesus will destroy him with the breath of His mouth and the splendour of His coming. Do you belong to God or do you belong to Satan, the enemy of God? It really matters who you belong to and that decision is yours alone to make and it carries eternal consequences.

In Ezekiel 33: 1-20, God appoints watchmen to sound the alarm when an enemy is coming to attack a nation. This is one of the roles of God's people, as God's watchmen, sounding the alarm to our nation. Ezekiel 33: 9, if you warn them to repent and they don't repent, they will die in their sins, but you will have saved yourself. God takes no pleasure in the death of anybody, even the wicked because He came down here to live among us and give us life. Why should we choose to die when we can choose to live? This is our watch, so may we be men and women of God sounding the alarm to prepare the people for the Enemies attack. Proverbs 17: 3.

2

PATTERNS FOR EVANGELISM

Philip is the only person in the Bible called a deacon or servant and an evangelist. Acts 21: 8-9 and Acts 6: 1-7. We are told he was an honourable, godly man full of wisdom and the Holy Spirit. He was chosen as one of seven men to serve the poor in Jerusalem during an outpouring of the Spirit after Pentecost. After a while Philip had to move away from Jerusalem after the murder of his brother Stephen at the hands of Saul, persecuting the Christians there. Nineteen years later we find him living in Caesarea with his four daughters all gifted in the prophetic. He was using his home to give hospitality to Apostle Paul, the same man who had murdered Stephen and chased him out of Jerusalem but now a believer himself. How amazing is the grace of God! Christian tradition tells us that Philip was one of the seventy sent out by Jesus in Luke 10. He is said to have been consecrated as a bishop by the Apostles and sent to Talles in Asia Minor where he died in his old age. This same tradition reports that his daughter Hermione served Christ by ministering to the sick, assisted by her sister Eukhidia. During Roman persecution Hermione was arrested and beheaded to become a Christian martyr.

Philip is a pattern evangelist to perfectly illustrate God's pattern for evangelism in these end times. He is a pattern and example to us all about what to expect in these end times. His pattern will be seen and emulated by many evangelists in the coming harvest of the nations. First of all, Philip was a man close enough to God to hear His voice and obey by partnering with angels and the Holy Spirit. He knew he had to depend on the resources of heaven to reap the harvest and he accessed every spiritual blessing in the heavenly realms. Ephesians 1: 3. It was an angel who told Philip to leave at noon down to the desert road that runs from Jerusalem to Gaza. This is the same notorious road Jesus spoke about where many were ambushed by bandits in Luke 10: 30-37. It was a dangerous place to be avoided unless absolutely necessary. Philip is ready to go without hesitation on hearing God's voice through the messenger angel as confirmed by the Holy Spirit in Acts 8: 26-29. Philip is strong and courageous not afraid or discouraged, he knows the Lord God is with him wherever he goes. Joshua 1: 9. Philip had placed himself at God's disposal and was ready to preach to crowds or individuals for the glory of God. He was ready to be in the public eye and ready to leave it as he travelled from Sebaste in Samaria to the desert road towards Gaza. He is carrying the heart of God for cities and individuals, a heart full of grace or love in action for the lost. He is the heart of an evangelist in action.

Philip also knew how to handle the Word of God. He used the Old Testament to show the treasurer his need of the Messiah, the One he was reading about in Isaiah the prophet. He used the Scriptures wisely under the guidance of the Holy Spirit to lead this African man to Christ, then baptise him in water. The Ethiopian man was probably the first African man to receive Christ and he was important and influential to the future spread of the Good News in Africa. Always obey God for the one because you never know what influence their saved life will carry for others. Philip shows we need to know God in the Old Testament to relate Him to the Messiah in the New. We must immerse ourselves in the whole Bible as Paul instructed Timothy in 2 Timothy 3: 14-17. We need to learn and see Christ in the Old and the New to be prepared and equipped for every good work.

Philip was strong, courageous and fearless in evangelism as he shared in Sebaste, which was under the demonic influence of the man

Simon Magus. Simon was a sorcerer and wizard who had boasted he was great and astounded many with his magic arts and occultic activities. Many of the people would be tormented and suffering as a result of Simon's dark magic. Philip draws attention to Jesus and promotes the power of the Good News and God begins to unravel the destructive influences of Simon. Many demon- possessed people are set free as evil spirits come out and many lame and paralysed people are healed. Acts 8: 5 tells us he preached the wonderful news of Jesus Christ, the Anointed One. Philip preaches the power of the cross and the blood of Jesus and many are saved, healed and delivered. He sets us a pattern to follow.

Next, Philip is translated supernaturally from one place to another to continue preaching the Good News. He was following the pattern of Ezekiel in Ezekiel 3: 12-15. Philip was moved a distance of about fifteen miles to Azotus to continue preaching to the crowds needing salvation. Because Philip had placed himself at God's disposal, he was ready and willing to be translated and go where God wanted him to be and God is looking for evangelists who are ready and willing, even to be translated to go where God wants them to be. Like Philip, God will use us to preach the Good News with signs and miracles which draw the crowds and break major occultic strongholds over cities and nations.

When people experience the power of God, they will flock to Him and leave the occult behind. Philip was a servant of the Lord, ready to obey and be led by the Holy Spirit. Get ready to serve God's end time plans in your community and see amazing things happen. Reach out to the one as well as the many and dedicate yourself to God as His evangelist.

Now we turn to another evangelist in John 4, a female led to God by Christ Himself and filled with rivers of living water. Jesus, is of course the greatest of all evangelists and here he shows us once again what it looks like to place yourself at God's disposal. Jesus has a divine appointment with a broken woman at a well in Sychar an area in Samaria. Christian tradition names the woman as Photini and she came to draw water at noon time, the hottest part of the day because she knew nobody would be there, it would be quiet because she had a bad reputation. She wanted to avoid other people because she struggled with sexual immorality and had been divorced five times and was now living in a relationship outside of marriage. She was a despised, rejected and broken woman as she crept out to the well on that desperately hot sunny day. God was looking at Photini differently, He saw her heart and reached out in love to her. Here is the grace of God or love in action as Jesus reveals the true nature of her God and Messiah and offers her forgiveness and rivers of living water. Jesus had begun to draw in the Father's harvest and Photini's testimony would bring many more to believe as her guilt and shame are removed by rivers of living water. She received new life, new hope and a new purpose and went on to share with many others including her community, family and even one of the Roman Emperor Nero's daughters, whom she led to Christ in Rome, where she was eventually martyred.

Photini's love for Jesus cost her everything but she died evangelising for her Master, who had met the deep love longing of her heart and given her a life worth living. She is another great pattern for evangelism left behind for us in the Scriptures. When we allow God to remove all our shame and guilt, we are set free to share with others and allow them the same freedom. Your story with God has the potential to set others completely free when you place yourself at His disposal from da on your journey with Jesus. Philip and Photini were two very different people but they had hearts so touched by God that they gave themselves completely to help others find Him. Will you do the same? Will you place yourself at God's disposal and follow His patterns for evangelism? May we all say yes to God and bring in the greatest end times harvest imaginable. John 4: 34-38.

We know much about Stephen, Philip and Photini but what about the other five deacons chosen to serve the poor in Jerusalem, they were a part of the magnificent seven? They are Prochorus, Nicanor, Timon, Parmenas and Nicholas the hero of Antioch. What became of these five men set apart to serve the Lord in Jerusalem? Again, we must rely on Christian historical tradition to learn about them. When the Apostles laid hands upon them it indicated approval, impartation of authority, commissioning and ordaining. They were now men appointed by God for serving and ministry. Hebrews 6: 2 and Acts 13: 2. It is interesting to note that fasting with prayers is considered to be a priestly duty and of service to the Lord. This means it is a ministry in its own right, very precious to the Lord and something many could be doing who may find themselves house bound. There is a ministry available to everybody in all circumstances today. Acts 6: 7 shows us that when God's Word reigns supreme and keeps spreading the number of people believing in Jesus increases, including the number of religious people, who had a form of religion but denied its power. The Jewish priests who became believers and were now obedient to the faith would have lost their jobs in the synagogues and been expelled from them. God could now use their priestly calling and knowledge to build His Church and provide for them and their families.

Prochorus was one of the seventy sent out by Jesus in Luke 10. His name means leader of a chorus and he was the nephew of Stephen the martyr. He was a companion to Peter and John and they ordained him to be the bishop of Nicomedia. He played a very important role in the development of early Christianity among Jewish and Samaritan converts. He did miracles in Jesus' Name and also became the bishop of Antioch where he died as a martyr in the first century.

Nicanor's name means conqueror and victorious. He was also one of the seventy sent out by Jesus in Luke 10. He suffered martyrdom in AD 76.

Timon was appointed by the Apostles as bishop of Bostra in Arabia. He was thrown into a furnace for preaching the gospel but by the power of God came out unharmed and well. He eventually died by crucifixion for his faith.

Parmenas preached the gospel in Asia Minor. He died in AD 98 as a martyr under the persecution of Trajan in Philippi. He became the bishop of Soli and his name means abiding or permanent.

Nicholas of Antioch was a proselyte or convert to the Jewish faith before his conversion to Christ. His name means victor of the people. He was the first non- Jew or Gentile to hold office in the Christian church. Some claim he was the founder of the sect called Nicolaitans, Revelation 2: 15, but others say this was a vain claim made by this sect in seeking apostolic authority for their opinions. Nicholas spoke Greek and had a Greek education and to become a proselyte he would have been circumcised, baptised and made a special gift to God at the Temple. He would have been devout and dedicated in his beliefs and must have had leadership qualities to have been chosen as a deacon as a Gentile. Antioch was the largest city and capital of the Roman province of Syria. It was multi-cultural with Greeks, Macedonians, Syrians, Jews, Romans and others. It was a mixture of languages, cultures, philosophies and religions.

3

MEN AND ANGELS, DREAMS AND VISIONS

The Lord God is Commander of the Angel Armies of heaven. He has an organized army of angelic beings in heaven, who are about to invade the earth in specific legions. What role do the angels have? The Bible tells us they are spirit-messengers sent by God to serve those who are going to be saved. Hebrews: 1:14. Angels were and are involved in your salvation. You may never see or hear them but they are there and they are actively involved in your life and mine. Angels, Holy Spirit and evangelists are being called to work together as a triple braided cord that cannot be broken. In Acts 8: 26 the Lord's messenger Angel gave Philip an assignment when he spoke to him. It was a simple instruction to be followed. Now or immediately, go south from Jerusalem on the desert road to Gaza. Philip didn't debate with the angel, he obeyed to the letter and as he went the Holy Spirit confirmed the message and even made it more specific. Go and walk alongside the chariot. Again, Philip obeyed and his faith opened the way for evangelism because he had been obedient to his heavenly assignment. Let us follow his example and train ourselves to be moved by the impulses of the Holy Spirit in whatever form they come.

Heaven's armies are organized, they have God given function, purpose and planning and we need to work with them to see the Kingdom of God established here on earth. There are breakthrough angels sent to work alongside God's intercessors and evangelists to powerfully preach the gospel message on earth and to break satanic strongholds from nations and communities. We see them working all around Peter and the crowds gathered to him on the Day of Pentecost when three thousand new believers are added to the church. Acts 2: 1-41. Gathering angels gathered the crowds to be in the right place at the right time, harvesting angels made it possible for the people to be baptized on the day they believed. The believers had met together to pray, the Holy Spirit was poured out and signs occur drawing the crowds, who are then harvested into the Kingdom of God and sealed by baptism. There is intense spiritual warfare going on involving angels, Holy Spirit and believers. This is always the way when it comes to salvation. There are angels of healing, miracles and revelation knowledge. There are angels who come as warriors to fight in the heavenly realms and on earth to defeat God's enemies and protect God's people. Exodus 14: 15-20; Psalm 91: 9-13; Psalm 103: 20-21; Daniel 8: 15-17; Daniel 9: 20-23; 2 Kings 6: 8-23.

The apocryphal book of Enoch tells us there are seven Archangels who are captains and generals over others. They are also called Watchers and they are named as Michael, Uriel, Raphael, Gabriel, Saraqael, Remiel and Raguel. In Hebrew the word El means God so these beings are angels of God sometimes called sons of God Most High. Uriel has authority over the visible world and the invisible world of Tartarus. Raphael has authority over the spirits of men. Raguel has authority over the stars and cosmic energies. Michael has authority over Israel, the best part of mankind and chaos. Saraqael has authority over spirits who sin. Gabriel has authority over paradise, the serpents and the Chrubim. Remiel has authority over the resurrection. All of these might beings are engaged in the worship of God in heaven but they are also engaged in prayer and intercession for those who dwell on the earth by fending off evil spirits. Michael is described as merciful and long suffering. Raphael also has authority over sickness and diseases afflicting men. Gabriel releases the power of God and an angel called Phanuel has authority to release repentance to those who inherit eternal life. God has anointed specific Archangels and angels as His messengers and authorities to govern and organize the created visible and invisible realms.

In Joshua 5: 13-15, Joshua is met by the commander of the Lord's Army. Joshua is told to worship before going into battle because he is standing in a holy place and about to inherit the promised land. In front of such a mighty being Joshua fell and worshiped God and the following day men and angels worked together to secure God's promises for Israel. Angels are sent to us with messages from heaven in the forms of dreams, visions, pictures and revelations. It is important to honour them and quickly write them down asking God for wisdom to understand them. The fire is coming and I want everybody to know it's coming, to be ready for it and to run with it. When the fire comes, some may try to extinguish it but that is not what God wants. He wants us to embrace it, run with it and spread it so that others will be touched and transformed.

Get ready for angelic assignments because when you embrace God's fire, He will assign you with heavenly tasks ordered by angels and anointed by the Holy Spirit. Place yourself at God's disposal night and day and you may even find yourself translated to share the Good News in different parts of the world. There is no limit to what God can do. With God all things are possible. I met somebody recently who told me they had a dream where they were translated to somewhere in China. It was a rural area well away from the city. They found themselves in a field and saw six farmers who had no Bible praying and they knew God wanted them to join their prayer gathering and share the Word of God with them. As he shared the farmers faces began to shine with the glory of God and he left them greatly inspired and encouraged with the Word of God. This is one example of what God can do if we are at His disposal. This person told me they really believed they had actually been to the place described as the whole experience had reality written all over it. Our dreams can be like trees of life if we take them more seriously and devote sleep time over to God. Hope deferred makes the heart sick but a dream fulfilled is a tree of life.

There are many stories of angels delivering God's messages to men in the Scriptures. Here are some of them, see if you can find more. Joshua 5: 13-15. Joshua receives strategy for taking Jericho from the commander of the angel armies. It was one commander sharing strategy with another in this instance.

Judges 3: 13-21. An angel visits Manoah and his wife to tell them she would bear a son. He also instructs them how the child was to be brought up, as a Nazirite from birth and his name was Samson.

Luke 1: 19-20. The Archangel Gabriel brings a message to Zacharias that his wife, Elizabeth would bear a son in her older age who would be the forerunner of the Messiah.

Luke 1: 18-27. Gabriel appears to Mary to announce her pregnancy with God's Anointed Son, to be named Yeshua or God of salvation.

Luke 2: 10. Angels announce the birth of the Messiah to the priestly shepherds, first one angel then a whole legion appears to be praising God. A legion is twelve thousand.

Matthew 1: 20; 2: 13; 19-20. Angels speak to Joseph in dreams guiding his decision making for himself, Mary and Jesus.

Matthew 28: 1-7. The resurrection of Jesus is proclaimed by angel, who also tells the disciples to meet the resurrected Messiah in Galilee.

Acts 1: 6-11. As Jesus ascends into heaven, two angels appear to tell His disciples He will return just as He has left them.

Revelation 2: 1- 3: 14. Seems to indicate every church age has an angel designated until Christ's return. This could also apply to every church in every church age, wherever Christian community gathers together for worship.

One thing is certain, when angels turn up the atmosphere changes and God's holy presence manifests and we become acutely aware of His glory, power and majesty. Angels stand in God's presence and bring it with them when they appear to us and it is an awesome presence like no other. I have had the privilege of three encounters with angels over the last fifty years of walking with God. They have had a profound effect on my faith. The first encounter was at an all- night prayer gathering in a friend's home. We were in the lounge praying for revival for Scotland and at 3am an angel exploded into the room knocking us both to the floor with our faces buried deep into the carpet. My friend was thrown from one end of the room to the other but not in any way hurt. I wanted to open my eyes but the fear of God had come upon me and I was just too afraid so I kept them shut as an overwhelming sense of God's holiness and my sin came over me. I was lying on holy ground and just repented from every sin I could think of as the presence of God filled the room. It was an awesome experience lasting for some time and now looking back I think it may have been a revival angel, who had come to assure us God had heard and would answer our prayers. We both agreed when it was all over that in some form God had come and was giving a foretaste of holy revival fire and it was awesome in every way.

The second and third encounters occurred in my bedroom in the deep of night and I was fully awake immediately. I looked up to see an angel hovering over the room and I watched huge wings beating up and down for at least twenty minutes. The angel was so big that the wings extended out of both sides of the bedroom and my heart was beating so loud and fast that I felt as if I might die. I saw this mighty angel once again under the same circumstances, weeks later. These encounters took place after God's prophets told me I was going to see angels. They were correct and I thank them for it. I am grateful to God for allowing me to see these angelic beings and to experience more of His presence and glory by being with them. God's supernatural, invisible world is full of awesome, powerful beings who carry the fearful and terrible presence of God, that is for sure.

Isaiah 6: 1-7. Woe is me. It's all over. I am doomed, for I am a sinful man. I have filthy lips and I live among a people with filthy lips. In the presence of God our guilt needs removed and our sins forgiven. The mighty seraphim have six wings and attend to the Lord as they call out to one another, holy, holy, holy, is the Lord of Heaven's Armies. The whole earth is filled with His glory. They are prophetic angels seeing into the future and declaring God's truth for the destiny of the earth. One day it will once again be completely filled with His glory as before. What a glorious day that will be for God and His beloved children as He is going to share this with us. Multitudes of angels are at God's disposal and He alone is worthy of worship and adoration. Why don't you take some time now to worship God and ask if He will allow you to be accompanied by angels to do so. They really know how to worship and can teach us a thing or two about it. One day soon we will worship God with them in glory. One day the new heaven and earth will be joined together in indescribable worship, love and adoration from angels and men. It will be loud and it will be wonderful and it's coming soon and suddenly. In God's presence is fullness of joy. At His right hand are pleasures forevermore. Psalm 19.

At this point I must say something about John 1: 14 where Jesus is described as being full of grace and truth. John 16: 10 also declares that righteousness has been made available to the human race now that Christ has come and died for us, then been raised from the dead. Grace comes before truth because God's love in action reaches down to us in all our lostness to save us from our sins. If truth came before grace, we would all be lost because truth is justice in action and we were condemned to die in our sins with no hope of salvation before Christ came to us. Christ makes righteousness available to the human race but we must receive it by faith in what He has done for us on the cross and by His resurrection life. But God shows His passionate love for us by dying for us when we were still lost, dead, weak, powerless and helpless. That is grace or God's riches at Christ's expense, God's love in action. All that God requires of us is satisfied by the sacrifice of Jesus on the cross. The Christ who is in us is enough to satisfy God. Grace means that anybody and everybody can be made right with God by receiving His forgiveness through genuine, lasting repentance or turning back towards Him. The thief who was repentant beside Jesus on the cross is a great example of saving grace. We need saving grace but also grace for newness of life throughout our Christian lives. Luke 23: 39-43. God's grace is available to our dying breath because God is gracious, merciful, slow to anger, full of unfailing love and faithfulness. He is compassionate and not willing that any should perish but all come to repentance.

Jesus has opened a door of grace before truth that will remain open until the full number of Gentiles comes in and all Israel are saved. Romans 11. But grace and truth also come together, first grace then truth. We need to remember this when sharing the Good News about Christ as we have a responsibility to tell people the truth about eternal things. People cannot reject God's grace and get away with it whether they describe themselves as believers or not. We must warn people about eternity and the judgement seat of Christ because it is the truth. We must be full of grace and truth in our evangelism to follow the example of Jesus. A gospel that is all grace without truth is not a balanced gospel and not the gospel of God. I hear many preaching a gospel of judgement on the city streets which seems void of grace but the opposite is also true. First let there be grace, then truth. 1 Peter 3: 13-17. We can learn to speak the truth with grace and love.

If we fail to speak the truth, we may leave the impression that God will allow so called good people into heaven because they have tried their best to be good. They are judging themselves by their own standards and not God's. But God has done everything required for people to be saved through what Christ has done on the cross. This is God's Way and it is good, perfect, right and powerful. It is just because the spotless blood shed by Christ alone can satisfy God's perfect justice. God wants people to hear about the cross and respond to it because we cannot save ourselves, it is His chosen Way of salvation. Human nature is sinful beyond human redemption, which is why Christ came as a sinless, spotless human and died a perfect sacrifice for us as fully human but also fully divine. The Son of God became the Son of Man so that sons of men might become sons of God. Our sinful human nature requires crucifixion and resurrection. Ephesians 2: 8-10. 2 Corinthians 5: 17.

We are continually being saved until Christ returns or we go to be with Him. People who say they are saved and then live lives in contradiction to the truth are actually living in denial of the truth and God has left us with warnings in Scripture to help us commit to Him and the truth. Hebrews 6: 4-8 and 10: 26-31. We must take responsibility to live lives that are pleasing to God because if we turn away from God's grace and truth, we have no further sacrifice available for sins. It is a false teaching to deny this truth. God calls us to a daily walk with Him, to carry our cross, fight the good fight, keep the faith and finish the race by crossing the finishing line faithfully. We are promised grace upon grace to be able to do this as we continue trusting in Him and His resources through the Holy Spirit.

We must stay alert and watchful because many may fall away in the last days deceived by false teaching and deception coming from Satan and his demons and not from God. Immerse yourself in the grace of God and His unfailing truth and continue walking with Him and work out your own salvation with fear and trembling. Philippians 1.

The King of glory is the Lord of Heaven's Armies and He sits enthroned behind the ancient gates and doors. Psalm 24. There is a gate in Jerusalem called the Golden Gate which is now inaccessible having being sealed over for many centuries. When the Messiah, The King of glory returns to sit on His throne on Mount Zion, He will once again pass through the Golden Gate. What a glorious moment that will be when the Golden Gate once again opens for the King of Glory to enter into His temple throne room. This sealed gate can only open for the Lion of the tribe of Judah and no other. It remains sealed until the appointed day of His triumphant return for He is strong, mighty and invincible in battle.

We need to hear a sound from heaven. We need flames and tongues of fire to appear and settle on each one of us. We need to speak about the wonderful things God has done. Who will step forwards in these last days to address the crowds? The Spirit is about to be poured out upon all people and sons and daughters will prophesy. Young men and women will see visions and older men and women will dream dreams. All of God's servants young and old are about to prophesy and release signs and wonders from heaven above to the earth below. Everyone who calls on the Name of the Lord will be saved. Death could not hold Him and it cannot hold us. The Lord is with us and we shall not be shaken for He is right beside us. Our hearts are glad and our tongues will shout His praises. Our bodies rest in hope for He has shown us the way of life and filled us with joy in His presence. Each one of you must repent of your sins and turn to God. Be baptized in the Name of Jesus Christ for the forgiveness of your sins, then you will receive the gift of the Holy

Spirit. This promise is to you and your children, to all who have been called by the Lord our God. It's time to share.

Remember Joseph. He had to wait two full years before the chief cupbearer remembered his encounter with him in prison. God's timing is absolutely perfect. Sometimes we need to wait patiently before our dreams come true. To wait on the Lord is never wasted time because He will use the time to entwine our hearts to His. Joseph's gift of dreams and interpretation had brought him before the most powerful king in the world at that time and now God was about to use him to interpret two of the king's troubling dreams. In the two dreams God was telling Pharaoh in advance what He was about to do over the next two decades. The king needed someone to manage the situation wisely to make full provision for what was coming. Joseph had just decreed a job for himself without knowing it. He had come from prison to power in one God moment where he finds himself exercising authority over the most powerful kingdom in the world at that time. There are Josephs out there whom God is preparing and equipping to share divine wisdom with secular leaders who will need supernatural help in the coming troubles. You may feel imprisoned and confined right now but your time to emerge and lead nations is coming so be encouraged and stand firm in your faith until God opens the ancient gates and doors to fulfil your destiny dreams. You are about to be promoted and step forward in these last days to address the crowds and to shape and guide the nations. Proverbs 15: 23; 18: 16; 20: 12; 25: 6-7; 28: 1-2; 31: 8-9.

God is giving His people dreams and visions to shape and guide the nations. Write them down and seek God until He makes sense of them in His appointed time. For the wise, these Proverbs will make you even wiser and for those with discernment, you will be able to acquire brilliant strategies for leadership. Proverbs 1: 5 TPT. The world and the Church are going to need God's brilliant strategies for leadership and the children are set to come forwards with them. This is God's wise way and He waits until we are ready and willing to receive from Him. Remember Joseph and dream as he dreamed. His dreams gave him hope to endure depressing situations for many years until at last when he was thirty, God delivered him from prison to power. His dreams became a tree of life providing nourishing fruit for him, his wife and family and all others in their season of greatest need. God used Joseph's gift to bring the world through a seven- year famine which was unprecedented. Joseph was a man who showed kindness to the poor and by doing so, he honoured their Maker. Proverbs 13: 12. He was a wise and faithful servant who received promotion from his king. Proverbs 14: 31. He was a man surrendered to the Lord, whom God could trust with revelation knowledge and Shekinah glory because of his sincere humility. Proverbs 15: 33. He may have made plans for his future but the Lord had chosen the steps to get there. Proverbs 16: 9. In the same way that gold and silver are refined by fire, the Lord purified his heart by the tests and trials of life. Proverbs 17: 3.

In Hebrews 2: 10-18 we are told that Jesus had to be a Man and take hold of our humanity in every way. He suffered and endured every test and temptation, so that He can help us every time we pass through the ordeals of life. In becoming human, Jesus fully identified with us and now He is our faithful and merciful King-Priest before God. He is one with us as we experience the tests and trials of life.

Who would have thought that the Covid 19 virus would bring whole nations to a standstill through the tests and trials of life and death exposing our immortality and vulnerability? Join with me in praying that many people will turn to God for hope, strength and courage during these difficult times where we need brilliant strategies for leadership to come through them. The words God gave to Joshua come to mind. This is My command, be strong and courageous! Do not be afraid or discouraged. For the Lord your God is with you wherever you go. Joshua 1: 9. What a verse to pray for doctors, nurses, carers and all front- line workers at this time. We thank God for them and continue to lift them up in our prayers for all they are doing for us.

4

YAH THE POWER OF GOD

Names are important so try your best to remember them. The Hebrew name for Stephen is Tzephaniah. In Hebrew the name means, Yah, has treasured him. Stephen was not an Apostle, yet he worked miracles of power through his ministry. The miraculous is not for the few but for the many so place your hand in God's and step out into the miraculous by faith in His Name and limitless power.

Zephaniah helps to answer the first of the many questions asked in the Bible. How can we escape if we neglect or ignore such a great salvation? This question is asked by the author of the book of Hebrews 2:3. It appears to be a quote from Deuteronomy 32:47.

Yah the God of power has treasured the prophet Zephaniah with a great, final end times revelation applicable to Jews and non-Jews all over the world. It is a call to repentance and gathering together to seek God and turn away from everything godless. It is a prophecy that is both terrible and fearful as it predicts global devastation on an incredible scale. Zephaniah's prophetic declaration would be considered harsh, judgemental and off the wall today but it is not, as even secular prophets of climate change are now declaring exactly the same thing from a secular and non-religious perspective. The truth is that nations who oppose the sure coming of the Kingdom of God will suffer the consequences because God rightly expects people to tremble at His Word, not completely ignore it. Nationalism is spreading all across the nations today as people groups try to establish their identity but without God our Creator and Redeemer, we have no identity. Nations may plunge themselves into wars, even civil wars in their search for identity. This is a danger for us here in Scotland as many persuade the nation into ever deeper conflict in an attempt to secure independence from the rest of the UK.

Glasgow can again flourish through the preaching of God's Word and the praising of His Name despite the city fathers feeling the need to change the God given motto decreed over us by Saint Mungo years ago. This is something worth protecting and crying out to God for, that it would be re-instated as our city motto. Standards of righteousness are being eroded daily all across the nation, which means we have to agree together to do something about it and cry out to God for His grace and mercy.

In Isaiah 12:1-6 we discover that God is coming to save, not to condemn or judge us. People imagine God to be distant but He is the One pursuing us not us Him. The whole of the Bible is a revelation about God's pursuing of us by coming down to us in the Person of His Son and offering Himself up for us to make us righteous. Because of what Jesus has done for us we can all be forgiven and made right with a holy God. This is the Good News of our gospel of grace. Why would anyone want to escape from such a wonderful God? His salvation is like a fountain or a well full of deep, living water and He invites us to come and joyfully drink from it daily. God's righteous anger against sin was poured out upon Jesus, His Beloved Son on the cross. At the cross the anger or wrath of God is satisfied because His justice is satisfied and an exchange can be made for anyone calling on His Name. Isaiah was looking ahead to the cross here and in chapter 53 where he sees the price being fully paid for our great salvation. We are now living in this wonderful day predicted by God's prophet Isaiah. How can we escape if we ignore such a great salvation?

This great salvation, which God holds out to us is always readily available, like the fountain the prophet saw and we must come and drink daily not just once. It is one reason it is described as a great salvation, it is a past, present and future experience for all who will come and drink. All three Persons of the Trinity of God are involved in the different aspects of our salvation. The Father saves us from the presence of sin. Jesus saves us from the guilt of sin. Holy Spirit saves us from the power of sin. See Psalm 2 TPT.

So, it was with our spiritual father Abraham in Genesis 12: 1-9, as he journeys on with God. Just as Abraham took Lot with him, we are to take others with us on our journey of faith to share together the blessings of God. In Genesis 12: 7 we are told the Lord appeared to Abraham and confirmed His promise to him and his seed. It may have been a vision, a dream or even a physical appearance, we are not specifically told but we know it was a divine encounter so real to Abraham that he built an altar in honour of God there to always remember it. This was Abraham's first salvation encounter with God but many more would follow throughout his journey of faith and so it must be with each of us. The Lord chooses to appear to us all in different ways but there is one thing each appearance has in common, we all know they are real and we remember each encounter by re-telling our stories or testimonies.

In this book you will read many such stories of how God has encountered people and set about transforming their broken lives step by step. They are modern day Abraham's and Sarah's. If you are an anyone, God is inviting you to come and drink from the fountain of His great salvation, Isaiah 55. All you need to be is thirsty and hungry to come and participate, to come and drink and eat. It is the best wine and the finest food as it strengthens us with life. God is offering us His unfailing love because He has a wonderful plan and purpose for each of our lives in Christ. His destiny dreams for us are glorious. He is inviting us into a covenant whereby He can display His power through us and empty all His promises into us. No wonder the writer to the Hebrews describes our salvation as great.

Like Abraham the prophet Isaiah saw the Lord, Isaiah 6:1-13. He remembers it as it was the same year king Uzziah died in 740 BC. Uzziah's death became his altar of remembrance. The prophet saw

God sitting on a lofty throne attended to by mighty Seraphim angels declaring His holiness and triune nature, Father, Son, Holy Spirit or holy, holy, holy. Heaven has its own special forces angel armies attending to God and being prepared to return to the earth with Christ to establish the Kingdom of God. They will enthrone Christ on Mount Zion in Jerusalem, where He will reign over the nations for one thousand years, then on into eternity.

When Isaiah saw the Lord, he expected to die because of his personal sin in the pure light of God's holiness but God becomes His Redeemer when He touches his lips with a burning coal from the altar, the place of sacrifice. Christ is our burning coal descending from the altar of God in heaven to touch and remove our guilt and forgive our sins. God saves His prophet and asks him two questions, two questions He still asks of us today. Whom should I send as a messenger to this people? Who will go for us? Isaiah 6:8. NLT. How will we respond to these questions? God is calling us to fulfil His Great Commission all across the earth today because Matthew 24:14 tells us that until we do, Christ will not return. When we truly see the Lord there is always response to Him. Abraham, Isaiah, Jeremiah all saw the lord and responded to Him obediently and so must we. Pray to the Lord of the Harvest to send out workers into His harvest fields, the world, and go as you pray in answer to your prayers.

Here are some other reasons why God's salvation is great. The Greek New Testament word for salvation is, "Sozo". It is used to describe healings, deliverances and faith in God or what we would call salvation. When Jesus healed the woman with the issue of blood the word used is sozo. Luke 8:43-48. Her faith in Jesus' ability and authority to heal her was her salvation. She had believed in Him enough to touch Him and be saved. Out of love Jesus asked her to share her story with the crowds because He knew it would bring many others, especially women into a right relationship with the God who saves. This was a broken woman despised by her community for an unclean disease and shunned by them until she met Jesus and everything changed. God is now bringing her back into the community on His terms, the terms of grace through faith in Jesus Christ. As Jesus drives out the Legion or six thousand demons from the demoniac the same word is used, sozo. Luke 8:26-39. Two people saved having experienced healing and deliverance following an encounter with Jesus. God's great salvation makes us right with God, heals and delivers us as we place our faith in all He has done for us on the cross. To encounter the risen Christ supernaturally is salvation, healing and deliverance. The atonement of Christ provides for humanities body, mind, soul and spirit. It is a full and complete or perfectly perfect atonement giving us full and complete salvation.

The present world is crying out to find meaning and the reality of the power of God. We must never deny people the opportunity to experience the fullness of Christ's perfect atoning work through the cross. People are suffering oppression everywhere from disease and demonic attacks and we have the answer to help save, heal and deliver them. The Hebrew name Yeshua or Jesus means Yahweh is our salvation, restoration and deliverance. O what a glorious Name and we are called by His Name, so let us apply the full meaning of it and preach the full gospel to this desperately needy world. We must try to represent Christ here on this earth fully not partially because we are His ambassadors.

In Proverbs 4: 20-23 we read that our whole bodies belong to God and He wants them to be radiantly healthy. As part of our great salvation God is validating our ministry with signs, astonishing wonders, all kinds of powerful miracles and by the gifts of the Holy Spirit according to His desire. May it be obvious that what we are doing is supernaturally blessed and authorised by heaven's kingdom realm. To settle for less than God's validation is dangerous because it can produce the fruit of religion without power and that is not New Testament faith in God. It is very easy to drift off course in this area and settle for less, much less than what God intends for us. If we preach a gospel devoid of the miraculous, we are neglecting to preach the fullness of our great salvation. The miraculous testifies to God's great salvation when people are transformed, healed, delivered and baptised in the power of the Holy Spirit. It is God's salvation and it is great, big, full, immeasurably more than all we can ask or imagine. Let us boldly preach His great salvation, a salvation capable of transforming hearts and minds, bodies, souls and spirits and turning whole communities the right way up in the Kingdom of God. Let us not settle for less than Father's very best.

What did it take and what did it cost for us to enjoy full and free access to God? Hebrews 10:20 tells us that just as the veil was torn in two in the Temple in Jerusalem, Jesus' body was torn open to give us free and fresh access to Father God in heaven. The full price has been paid by Jesus for us to come through His sacred blood sacrifice. Jesus is our Great High Priest who welcomes us into God's House to come close to God with open hearts that are clean, unstained and acceptable to God. Our hearts are sprinkled with His holy blood to remove all impurity and our consciences free from accusation. O how wonderful is the sinless, spotless, faultless, blameless blood of Jesus. It speaks for us in heaven today, bringing us close to God to worship Him in Spirit and truth.

There is a wonderful verse in Hebrews 10: 14 NLT. By His one perfect sacrifice, He, Christ, forever made perfect those who are being made holy. How can we be made perfect and still not be completely holy? The answer is the author is speaking about two different aspects of our salvation namely justification and sanctification. Here God is clearly saying that Christ's perfect sacrifice saves us completely and forever because it is perfect and needs no improvement or addition. However, we are continually being made holy or sanctified until the day we enter heaven and become like Christ in every way.

When Christ enters your heart by faith you are justified or found not guilty in the courtroom of heaven because of His perfect blood cleansing sacrifice for you, when He died in your place. His sacred, holy, blameless, faultless, innocent blood washes away all and every one of all your sins. God kisses your heart with His forgiveness in spite of all you have done and because of all that Christ has done for you. Christ is your Life- Giving Saviour from the second you repent before God and receive Him into your life and that means His forgiveness and righteousness are exchanged for your guilt and sinfulness at the cross.

We must be careful not to get justification and sanctification mixed up because they are two different things as taught by this marvellous truth in Hebrews 10.

God's great salvation means we are acquitted by God and found not guilty or justified in the courtroom of heaven where the sacred blood of Christ His Beloved Son is presented to Him on our behalf and accepted as our saving sacrifice forever. This wonderful truth is eternal and unchangeable because it is a grace covenant made with us by God Himself on the basis of what Christ has done for us. When we accept this by faith, we enter into a new living relationship with God which is eternal and perfect. David knew all about these things even under the old covenant when he wrote Psalm 103 for us. He asks how can I ever forget the miracles of kindness You have done for me? He then goes on to thank and praise God for each miracle of kindness throughout the psalm but especially in verses 1-5. He is praising God for His forgiveness in spite of all he has done and this is grace. He is thanking God for healing him inside and out, rescuing him from hades and saving his life. He is worshiping God for crowning him with His love and mercy.

David is celebrating the Father's love for us throughout this wonderful psalm of praise and worship to God. He is celebrating the truth that it is the Father's passionate love for us that pursues us all the days of our lives and not our love for Him and this is very liberating. His love is like a flooding river overflowing its banks with kindness.

The heart of God is greatly saddened by people rejecting His love for them when they scorn the blood of the cross that could save them and mock God's Spirit of grace. How can we escape when we ignore or reject such a great salvation? There are people reading this who are unsure if they are saved because they have become confused about salvation and sanctification. I assure you right now that when you turn to God, repent from sin and receive Christ by asking Him into your life you are saved forever. Christ's work for you on the cross is complete and perfect so you can depend on what He has done for you completely because you are complete in Him. Take responsibility to remain in Him and allow the Holy Spirit to save you from the power of sin, just as Christ saves you from the guilt of sin. Christ's blood sacrifice continually washes us from sin's guilt, presence and power. 1 John 1: 6-7. Justification occurs in a moment but sanctification takes a lifetime and you can be sure that God will complete and finish every good work He begins in you. Philippians 1: 6, 2: 13-14.

In the Passion Translation Hebrews 10:18 is a question. So, if our sins are forgiven and forgotten why would we need to offer another sacrifice for sin? There is no need to offer God another sacrifice for sin because Christ's sacrifice is perfect and complete. We must trust in it perfectly and completely to be saved. If you are a believer and struggle with sins from your past already repented from, it is time to realise God has forgiven and forgotten so you must do the same. I spoke to somebody recently being tormented by a sin from his past through recurring nightmares coming from Satan. He would wake up in a cold sweat reliving the particular sin over and over unsure if he could be forgiven for it. But then God spoke to him through Psalm 103 telling him He had kissed his heart with forgiveness in spite of what he had done. The grace of God broke through and he received God's forgiveness joyfully through the assurance given by God Himself in His Word. The devil can be the source of this problem or our own pride or even other people but none of them have the right to speak condemnation over us when God forgives and forgets. It is a question of who we give authority to as far as healing and redemption or condemnation is concerned.

God's family are all blood bought. With His blood He purchased us, on the cross He sealed our pardon, paid our debts and set us free. Rest in Christ's purchase, pardon and full payment for you today as you are adopted and chosen as God's holy child. There is a newly-slain, life-giving way opened up for us to approach God our Father in the most holy sanctuary of the heavenly realm. It is through the sacred life blood of Jesus our Messiah. Nothing can keep us at a distance from God, who welcomes us into His house sprinkled with blood, pure, clean, unblemished in His sight. Now we are clean, unstained and presentable to God inside and out.

What about people who were at one time thought to be believers but now choose to persist in deliberate sin, having known and received the truth? Hebrews 10: 26-31 seems to answer this question. They are living in total denial of everything Christ has achieved for them and therefore placing themselves under the judgement of God, rather than the grace of God offered freely to them. It is not enough to know and receive God's truth, we must obey and choose to walk in union with Christ daily. Jesus commanded us to take up our cross daily and follow Him in order to become fishers of men. It costs and demands an appropriate response in other words.

We must remember we are living in perilous, occultic and demonic times. We must take personal responsibility to walk with God and remain in Christ under His grace. If Jesus is our Lord, then He is Master and Owner which means we are under His authority and expected to be obedient to Him. We need to use our faith, learn to endure and love as Christ loves. This is something God expects from us all as His sons and daughters, called as ambassadors in a hostile world. He has given us the Holy Spirit to fill us with His love. Romans 5: 1-5. Times of trouble are here with more coming as light and darkness together cover the earth. Isaiah 60:1-3. God will use times of trouble to build Christlike character into us and release His endless love through us. We confidently and joyfully look forward to sharing God's own glory.

2 Corinthians 5: 17. Now if anyone is enfolded into Christ, he has become a new person. All that is related to the old order has vanished. This includes our old identity, our life of sin, the power of Satan, the religious works of trying to please God, our old relationships with the world and our old mind-sets or patterns of thought keeping us in bondage to sin. Behold, everything is fresh and new or a new order has come into our lives, God's order. And God has made all things new and reconciled us to Himself, and given us the ministry of reconciling others to Himself. We are ambassadors of the Anointed One, who carry the message of Christ to the world, as though God were tenderly pleading with them directly through our lips. For God made Christ, who never sinned, to become sin itself and the offering for our sin, so

that we could be made right with God through Christ. 2Cor 5: 17-21 TPT Notes and NLT.

Don't be a believer full of unbelief. Instead, be full of the Holy Spirit and glorify God through your faith, confidence and trust in Him. Jeremiah 17: 5-10 describes two very different people. One is likened to a stunted shrub in the desert with no hope for the future. The other to a tree planted along a riverbank with roots reaching deep into life-giving water. Will you be a stunted shrub or a deeply rooted tree? The tree has rich green leaves and delicious fruits no matter what the weather throws at it because it is anchored in the unseen realm of the Kingdom of God the life- giving water. Jesus is our fountain of life-giving water inviting us to come and drink from Him daily and even moment by moment. He is also our evergreen, fruitful tree. Such trees are not bothered by the heat or worried by long months of drought. Are you in a season of heat and drought in your journey with God right now? Do not despair, He is promising you that even now He will keep your leaves fresh and lush and you will never stop producing fruit. It is good to take this Word from God and declare it out loud over your life right now and your words have the power of life to bring about what God is promising you.

Church tradition from Jewish historians records the woman at the well in John 4 as Photini, a Samaritan woman from Sychar in what is now the West Bank. When she met Jesus, she had little hope for her future because she had failed relationships in her pursuit of love and identity. Jesus saw right into the depths of her heart where He saw a woman disappointed and empty, yet still searching for the highest form of love. God's great salvation is the highest form of love. Human beings were created by God to know, experience and enjoy His Hooba-Agape love. This kind of love is fiery, zealous, passionate, the highest and best love of God for us His sons and daughters. It is a love providing us with constant hope and security, which tolerates no rivals, a jealous love. It is a love that draws us to Himself when we feel lost and empty like Photini at the well. When Photini drank from the living fountain of Jesus she was transformed to become all God had planned she could be in Christ. Jesus had satisfied that God designed space in her heart that only He can satisfy. She went on to become a mighty Apostle and evangelist leading many other empty ones to her Saviour. She brought the message of salvation to her sisters and two sons as well as her whole village before travelling to Rome where she brought one of Nero's daughters to Christ. She is a glorious picture of an end times Church moving outwards in victory like the Warrior Bride of Proverbs 31. We are now His end times great Warrior Bride in union and unity with Him and one another committed to taking His witness to the world that is soon and very suddenly passing away. May we take His great salvation out into His world and elevate Him to His rightful place as Lord and Judge of all mankind.

1 Corinthians 3: 5-11 may be thinking about Solomon's Temple which was built using gold, silver and precious, costly stones. Gold represents divine substance or character, silver represents redemption's fruits, costly stones represent the transformation of broken lives by God's superabundant grace and power. Wood, hay and stubble or straw are emblems of the works of the flesh, the building materials of men, not God. They grow up from the ground, which God cursed, Genesis 3: 17. God commends quality and durability. Fire will cause the better material to glow brighter, but the inferior material will be consumed. How we build and what we build matters to God. God's work needs to be done God's way. We will look at this in the next chapter after we hear the wonderful stories of some costly, precious stones.

5

C'S STORY

Hi my name is C. I work with people who have life controlling problems. My life before I met with God was chaotic to say the least. I grew up in a good family home where I was loved. I have many good memories of my upbringing. Even though there was good going on in my life I started to go down the wrong path. I chose this path and only looking back now do I wish I knew the outcome or should I say listened to people telling me the outcome!

I thought I knew it all but how wrong I was. I started using drugs at 14 and this was just the start of all my problems. I would rob and steal to find money to buy drugs. This went on for a number of years and along the way I discovered alcohol and other heavier drugs.

I lived to party and I used to say I lived for the weekends. By the age of 33 my life was a mess. My mental and physical health were badly affected by my lifestyle. The bad times started to outweigh the good as I came to the end of myself. Broken on the inside and crying out for help I walked through the doors of a church. Looking back, I believe and know God put a pull on my heart to walk through those doors.

I tried something new and made a positive life changing decision that impacted my life right from the start. God started loving me through the people in the church. I had to go away to deal with my addiction issues and address the stuff going on inside. I came to a place where I recognised my need for God because I felt a void in the inside that I had been trying to fill with all the wrong stuff. Once I started filling it with the right stuff and coming to a place where I could find God, things have never been the same.

Yes, life is tough at times and can challenge you, but I know and have learned that as long as I am living in a relationship with God through His Word, I am in a better place to make better choices. He gives me the strength to get through trying times, something I never had before. I give God all the glory for this. Ecclesiastes 3: 11 Amplified Version. Permission given by C for his story.

6

FOUR GODLY MEN

In this chapter I want to look briefly at the lives of four men of God in the Bible, Joshua, Isaiah, Jeremiah and Daniel.

God called Joshua to be a strong and courageous leader just like his mentor Moses had been. To be successful and prosperous Joshua must study and meditate on the words of God given to Moses in the Torah on Mount Sinai. God's word would create faith in Joshua to be obedient and carry out all God would be asking him to do to complete the work of Moses and bring His chosen people into the promised land. Big battles would be necessary so Joshua would need to be strong and courageous and full of faith. We are no different. We must meditate on God's word, old and new covenants to receive the faith we need to finish the work God has set aside for each of us in His Kingdom realm. There is a tendency today for people to ignore the Old Testament but this is damaging to our faith and growth as children of God for there are hidden treasures waiting for us to discover in both. I remember reading Victorious Christian Living by Dr Alan Redpath as a young believer and it really blessed me at the time through studies in Joshua.

As mentioned in chapter one, in 740 BC Isaiah had a powerful and life changing encounter with God. He remembers it as the year King Uzziah died. He finds himself standing before God in a Temple where

God is enthroned with two seraphim angels beside Him. Even these mighty seraphs are not permitted to look directly at God as they have two wings to cover their faces and feet and another two used to fly. These seraphs are declaring the holiness of God in heaven and that He is triune and leader of a heavenly army. The seraphs seem to see into the future when they declare the whole earth to be filled with the glory of God. This is most powerful as it gives us a glimpse into our future where we will joyfully and confidently share God's glory. Romans 5: 2. The voices of the seraphim are so powerful and thunderous that the Temple is shaken to its foundations and filled with smoke. Isaiah is overwhelmed with the holy fear of God and feels he may die unless he is assured his sin is forgiven and washed away. God sends one seraph to atone for him from the altar which is a picture of the cross and Calvary. The prophet's guilt is removed and he is forgiven by God's sacrifice for him from His altar in heaven. God is asking for people to represent Him on earth by becoming His messengers and taking His message out to others in need of it. God sends him out with the message and He will do exactly the same for us should we agree to go as Isaiah. God's message to Isaiah is a message ending in hope for all who will receive it from him. Isaiah 6: 1-13 NLT.

God's messengers must be faithfully willing to deliver God's messages and not their own. For Jeremiah this meant opposition and persecution because the people were unwilling to receive it. He remained faithful despite being thrown into jail and intimidated by the nations governing rulers. Daniel read Jeremiah's prophecy and responded to it and because of this obedience God gave him an end times vision and revelation for His people. Daniel lived in the present and the future as God showed him both realms and made them real to him. In Daniel and the book of revelation we see God speaking in sevens, this is His love language to us. Israel had been in captivity for one set of sevens or seventy years and God told Daniel the Messiah would come after another 69 sevens. We know the Messiah has come and now we are waiting for the final seven when the ruler and defiler will come during the final seven- year period called the tribulation or Jacob's trouble. I believe God is currently preparing His people for this time. When Israel signs a seven- year peace treaty which is violated after three and a half years we will know the age of men is coming to a close. Daniel has passed his revelation onto our generation to run with it and carry the baton across the line. I thank God for the wonderful faith of these four very different Hebrew men and the impact it can have on our lives of faith today when we read all about them. The Word of God they have placed in our hands is tried, tested and true. We must run with it by holding onto it firmly and running in the Spirit towards the finishing line.

God's great salvation needs to be preached with love and tenderness to bring many broken people into His loving, healing arms. Let me tell you about three people who have encountered the love of God recently on the city streets, their names have been changed to protect their privacy.

They are a small part of the mighty harvest of souls God is presently bringing into His Kingdom realm. We met Reggie in Queen Street outside the Gallery of Modern Art leaning against the cone headed statue infamous in Glasgow. He had just been in a fight with somebody who had insulted his dead mother who had been murdered when he was ten years old. He shared his painful memories about his mum at such a tender age and the tears poured down his bleeding face. An anointed mother on our team hugged and held him to comfort and bless him as he spoke to us. He told us about God's grace and mercy in his own life when he had been knocked down by a car and had survived being in a coma and terrible leg injuries. He had been given the last rites in hospital by a priest known to his family. We asked him if he died tonight, did he know for sure he would go straight to heaven? He did not know so we prayed with him and he invited Christ into his life to forgive and change him from the inside out. He was a broken man experiencing the love and acceptance of Christ for the very first time in his pain filled life. What joy filled the courts of heaven as another lost son is brought into the loving arms of his heavenly Father.

We met A in Argyle Street. She was angry with God for taking her daughter into heaven when she was just twenty years old. She felt cheated and let down by God. Alice wanted assurance she would see her daughter again so we shared God's Way into heaven through the blood of Jesus shed on the cross and she immediately accepted Him. She opened her brokenness to Jesus asking Him for forgiveness and healing to trust Him for her own future and her daughters.

D had practiced the Moslem faith for many years as a convert but it had left him lonely and empty inside. He was thirsty for more and reaching out to God for answers. As we listened to him in Gordon Street, he told us he had been watching as we loved the homeless there. Derek had turned to drugs to ease the pain in his soul but this had also left him empty and hungry for an encounter with the Living God of Abraham, Isaac and Jacob. He knew the bible story of how God had prevented Abraham sacrificing his own son Isaac by providing a lamb in his place on Mount Moriah. As we spoke to him, he suddenly realised that Jesus Christ was the same Lamb sacrificed for him at Calvary and on making that vital connection he invited Christ into his life to save and wash away his sins. What joy as he experienced his emptiness being filled by the love of God. There is a vast harvest ripe and ready to come into God's eternal Kingdom but we need more willing to answer God's call to get out there and bring it in. Will you say yes to God and start to share your faith with the lost and dead to awaken them to eternal life? Will you say Lord send me I will go just as Isaiah after his encounter with God? God will give you His message for them when He sees your willingness to respond to His call, wherever it may be.

How are we going to respond to the two questions God asks us through His prophet Isaiah? Our motivation to respond must be because we know and experience Christ's love for us. I want us to look at the many loves Jesus and the Father have for us beginning in Ephesians 3:14-21, one of Apostle Paul's great prayers for the Church. Christ's love for us is to become the resting place and root and source of our lives. It is vital we learn to rest in Christ's love for us, rather than ours for Him. In Romans 5:8, we see that God proved His passionate love for us by sending Christ to die in our place on the cross. But Christ did this when we were lost, ungodly, weak, powerless and helpless. God's unconditional love for us, which we could never earn or deserve is given to us in what Christ has done for us, if we choose to believe and accept it. Christ has done everything necessary to save mankind even to the point of becoming sin itself, despite never sinning Himself, as our perfectly complete sacrifice to satisfy God's justice and righteousness. 2 Corinthians 5:21. I cannot think of better news, it is just simply marvellous, what God has done for us in Christ.

Surely our response to God for His sacrifice should be to praise and thank Him and live the rest of our lives serving Him in gratitude for it. Psalm 96 seems to indicate the kind of response God is looking for from us. Christ's passionate love for us is intense, strongly emotional and enthusiastic. Let us respond to Him in like manner for all He has done and continues to do in us.

Christ's love for us is endless, consistent, unaffected by time and eternity. Romans 5:5, TPT. Paul goes deeper into this at the end of Romans 8, when he reveals that nothing in all creation can separate us from the endlessly, passionate, love of Christ for us.

Christ's love for us is unfailing, Romans 5:9. This means it is continuous and reliable because God is love. Christ's love for us is excellent because He is outstandingly good at loving us, as befits His royal standing.

Christ's love for us is astonishing as it surely surprises us and overwhelms us with amazement.

Christ's love for us is deeply intimate, Psalm 139 from beginning to end reveals this in a most wonderful way. He loves us deeply, closely and very personally in a two- way relationship that is private to every one of us. We were created to experience the deeply intimate love of Christ personally because it has the life of God in it like nothing else and nothing satisfies us like the life of God. Psalm 63:5.

Christ's love for us is far reaching because it continually reaches out to every human being to give us meaning, value and significance. He alone tells us why we are here and where we are going after we die. His love reaches out far beyond this life into eternity to help us to become eternally secure in His love for us forever.

Christ's love for us is inclusive as it includes everything and everyone created who will repent and turn back towards Him for the forgiveness of their sins. It is love which motivates creation and re-creation.

Christ's love for us is beyond measurement or measureless because it is not meant to be measured but received by faith. It is designed to be experienced not measured as no words can measure something measureless. It is beyond our understanding therefore given to be experienced by the human body, soul and spirit. Ephesians 3: 18-19, TPT.

Christ's love for us is extravagant because it wants to fill us until we are filled to overflowing with the fullness of God.

These are just thirteen of the distinct qualities or virtues of Christ's many loves for us and I would ask you to meditate on each one until it becomes a reality in your life. Then you will be resting in His love for you and it will become the very root and source of your life.

In Psalm 62: 12, God declares that all the love we need comes from Him. He calls us to experience His love so that we can love as He loves. 1 John 3 and 4. I think Paul was moved by the Holy Spirit to write 1 Corinthians 13: 1-13, so that we would make Christ's agape love the motivation of our lives and the beautiful prize for which we run and fight the good fight. When we begin to experience Christ's many loves for us, we are transformed into His image and likeness. Faith and hope are temporary but love is eternal and faith and hope spring from love, therefore love is the greatest of all virtues in the kingdom of God.

This love that Christ deposits within us is loyal to the very end, even if the end is not quite as glamorous as we had imagined. God knows our beginning and end and He loves us, so we can trust Him and remain loyal to Him. It is a love done with fear of punishment, as fear is exchanged for peace with God. With His blood He purchased us, On the cross He sealed our pardon, He paid our debt and made us free. We are purchased, pardoned and paid for adopted sons of God forever loved by Him.

In Psalm 139:17 TPT, we are told we are cherished by God in His every thought. God is unique as far as this ability is concerned because it is extravagant love of the Father for His children never out of His thoughts even for a millisecond. To cherish is to hold dear, nurture, shelter and support. It is to sustain, treasure, care for, comfort and nurse. This truth about our heavenly Father is precious and wonderful to consider. Every single moment, Father is thinking about us with cherishing thoughts and desires that are more than the grains of sand on the seashores. The intimate depths of God's many loves for us are limitless. It will take an eternity to explore the fullness of His endless loves.

The resting place of God's many loves for us is our place of safety and encouragement in the stormy seas of life. In Song of Songs 1: 2, we have a beautiful verse describing God's revelation of His many loves. He wants to continually kiss us again and again and His kisses represent His different loves such as His saving love, keeping love, forgiving love and embracing love. We are to drink in God's many loves like the sweetest wines imaginable. The Hebrew word for kiss is NASHAQ, which can also mean to equip, or to arm for battle. God is kissing us again and again to arm us for battle as His warriors, set apart for Him. God feels passionate, fiery love for us, which must be shown or demonstrated permanently. As Holy Spirit kisses you with God's divine Word you will receive a new fresh revelation of His love equipping you as His warrior intoxicated by His love.

All God requires of us is satisfied by the sacrifice of Jesus Christ on the cross. The Christ in us is enough to satisfy God. In the courtroom of heaven, we are justified or declared not guilty by God our Judge as He sees Christ's blood sacrifice and acquits us from all guilt and sin because of it. This is the only way any human being can enter heaven or the Kingdom of God, through Christ's perfect and complete sacrifice, never through any righteous deeds of our own. Praise God for His awesome grace and mercy poured into us through Jesus Christ our Lord. Take some time today to open your Bible at Psalm 103 and with your heart, soul and innermost being worship God for all He is doing for you. Bow in wonder and love before your holy God and celebrate Him and His love for you.

His love is such that He kisses your heart with forgiveness in spite of all you have done. He does it because of what He has done, not you. Recently I spoke to a new believer who was having nightmares because he had killed somebody years before and struggled to know if God could forgive him for what he had done. He did not know that Moses,

David and Saul were all murderers forgiven and used by God. He was totally liberated by God's forgiveness in spite of all he had done, which is the promise of God in Psalm 103 TPT. He started to realise that the cross was powerful enough to wash away his personal sin no matter what he had done. This is our God, there is nobody outside of His love, grace and mercy following repentance and turning back to Him. It is a message filled with love that this world needs to hear through you.

God's love is like a flooding river overflowing its banks with kindness. Greater than the grandeur of heaven above is the greatness of His loyal love, towering over all who fear Him and bow down before Him. He removes our guilt and shame from us as far as east is from west, which is an eternal distance because there is no pole at east or west, as there is at north and south.

And now all glory to God, who is able to keep us from falling away and who will bring us into His glorious presence with great joy and without a single fault. All glory to Him who is God our Saviour through Jesus Christ our Lord. All glory, majesty, power and authority are His before all time, in the present and beyond all time. Amen. Jude 24 NLT.

A helpful prayer for God's love and forgiveness:

Heavenly Father thank You for loving me passionately despite what I have done. Please accept my turning away from all sin and accept me because of what Christ has done for me on the cross. I give my whole life to You now to serve You the remainder of my days and to help others find Your great forgiveness and grace. Thank You that Christ's sacrifice means that there is nothing I have done that I cannot be forgiven for after turning away from it towards You. Fill me now with the Holy Spirit to show me how much you love me and anoint me as one of Your beloved warriors. Thank You for saving me by Your grace and mercy in Jesus' Name, Amen.

7

THE CROSS

C entral to the ministry of Jesus is His death and crucifixion which is why the cross is the universally recognised symbol of the Christian faith. It is His cross that reconciles us to God. There is no gospel without the cross. As Jesus is portrayed as our crucified Saviour, Anointed One, Life- Giver the cross gives the message power and authority from heaven to save. The good news of the gospel is that through Jesus' atoning death and victorious resurrection, we have been given new life.

The great revelation of the cross has been supernaturally given to us but we must not dilute the glorious work of the cross by adding to it the works of religion. When we believe in Messiah, we are given the gift of the Holy Spirit from God. New life begins with the Holy Spirit giving us new birth. New life is living in the Holy Spirit. The Holy Spirit is poured out upon us through the revelation and power of faith. Abraham believed and received long ago and he became our pattern of faith. Genesis 15: 6. Habakkuk 2: 4, tells us that those who have been made holy will live by faith. And now God gives us the promise of the wonderful Holy Spirit, who lives within us when we believe in Him and uses the Word of God to increase our faith. Sadly, many people calling themselves believers are restricting the Holy Spirit's faith ministry to them by dismissing parts of the Scriptures as no longer applicable and this is to their eternal loss.

We must listen to and obey God more than pleasing religious leaders just as the first believers had to when confronted by religious legalism. Acts 5: 27-32.

Paul explains that we have died to sin once and for all, as a dead person passes away from this life. So, he asks, how can we live under sin's rule a moment longer? When we are baptised into union with Jesus, we are immersed into union with His death. When we are baptised, we are sharing in the death of Jesus Christ, as we are co-buried and entombed with Him, so that we can be raised with Him and walk in the freshness of a new life in the Holy Spirit. The old son of Adam identity within us is now deprived of its power, as the stronghold of sin is dismantled within us and sin is put out of business in our lives. Sin is cancelled and made redundant by the power of the cross for it has been forever crucified. Galatians 2: 20. Christ is our new Life- Giver and we are called to share in the fullness of His life. We can now live continuously for the Father's pleasure united to Christ. It is time for God's holy Church to live daily for God's pleasure in union with Jesus the Anointed One.

Galatians 2: 20 is a marvellous verse in the passion translation describing the meaning of Jesus' crucifixion. "My old identity has been co-crucified with Messiah and no longer lives; for the nails of His cross crucified me with Him. And now the essence of this new life is no longer mine, for the Anointed One lives His life through me, we live in union as one. My new life is empowered by the faith of the Son of God who loves me so much that He gave Himself for me, and dispenses His life into mine". Does Jesus' crucifixion mean this to you? Are you the new person God has re-created you to be in Christ? Is your new life daily empowered by the Son of God? He loves you so much that He gave Himself for you and wants to dispense His life into yours through the Holy Spirit. This is the meaning of Jesus' crucifixion, it is also our crucifixion to our old identity, our old sinful thoughts, ways and habits. We cannot be the same anymore in union with our Life-Giver and Anointed One.

If you have been genuinely saved by God then your old life must be crucified as you are raised to a new way of living in union with Jesus Christ through the power of the indwelling Holy Spirit. When Jesus saves us, we are resurrected through the washing of re-birth. We are made completely new by the Holy Spirit, whom He splashed over us richly by Jesus the Messiah, our Life- Giver. So, as a gift of His love, and since we are faultless, innocent before His face, we can now become heirs of all things, all because of an overflowing hope of eternal life. Titus 3: 6-7.

We must reveal Jesus to others as the crucified One in order for them to be saved according to the Scriptures for there is no other way to be saved. Acts 4: 12. If you were led to Christ without hearing the message of His being crucified for you, then you have heard a different gospel message and may not be saved. I pray that God would reveal His love to you today through the cross where He did it all for you.

In 1 Corinthians 15: 1-11, Paul is declaring the heart of the gospel, the only revelation given by God for us all to be saved. To be saved we must fasten our lives firmly to God's message and believe it because salvation is past, present and future therefore we have a continuous need for it in our lives. The gospel message is of utmost importance and he lays it out clearly for us in verses 3-5. The Messiah died for our sins on the cross, fulfilling the Scriptures such as Psalm 22, Psalm 16, Isaiah 52:13-53:12. He was buried in a tomb and was raised from the dead after three days as foretold in the Scriptures, Psalm 16: 9,10; Luke 24: 25-27 and 44-46. To believe these things is to believe the gospel and to preach is to preach Christ crucified and raised from the dead. There is no other true saving gospel other than this glorious message of good news passed down to us from the Lord Himself and the Apostles and Prophets called out from this world into His Church. We must remain faithful to this gospel and avoid changing the emphasis away from the cross.

There are many other gospels being promoted in the world today but none of them can save because they are empty, false and godless. They fail to expose the real root of mankind's problem, which is sin and our need for forgiveness from God. We meet people regularly on the street who have no awareness or consciousness of personal sin until we share the Scriptures with them. Without conviction of sin people feel no need for a Saviour and sometimes it is our role to help them understand this to come to Christ. There can be no end times great outpouring and revival without an awareness of sin and its remedy at the cross. Today sin is being made acceptable, tolerable and even desirable by those who deny God's existence and refuse to accept the authority of the Bible. They want to take us away from God and His values into darkness and death as they walk away from the light of the cross. We must stand as God's holy lovers to reverse this trend and preach its power to save, heal and deliver.

We are heading into an end times scenario whereby mankind will do everything possible to turn away from the cross but we must not allow this to happen by remaining faithful to preach it right to the very end. It is our joy and responsibility to continue writing the only book in the Bible left unfinished, the Book of Acts. We can only rise to this challenge by preaching the cross in the power of the Holy Spirit expecting God to confirm the message with supernatural signs, wonders and miracles and the gifts of the Holy Spirit. If you are one of the believers I mentioned earlier struggling with the ministry of the Holy Spirit, I can honestly say to you that without Him you will never remain faithful to the message of the cross. The end times will be full of counterfeit supernatural events that can only be exposed by the real thing as we step out in faith and release them into society because people are hungry and thirsty for the supernatural and the whole gospel is supernatural from beginning to end.

Do not allow your lack of experience to form your doctrine of the Holy Spirit when He is waiting for you to surrender all to Him and fill you like never before. If Jesus and the disciples needed the Holy Spirit, so do we and it is completely unbiblical to think and act otherwise. To move around witnessing for Jesus without the full anointing of the Holy Spirit through unbelief is like going into battle with your hands tied around your back, I don't recommend it. Come before Him now and make a new commitment to serve Him in partnership and in faith according to the Scriptures not your experience.

Today we need to become like those believers were on the Day of Pentecost as they prayed together, shook their nation and spoke the word of God with unrestrained boldness. The Greek word used here is "parresia" and means more than confidence, it means a free-flowing unrestrained boldness and freedom of speech to say anything on your mind. It is speech with no restraint, it is heart flowing, frank and honest, hiding nothing and speaking directly to the heart. It refers to speech that is not tailored to make everyone happy but to speak the truth, in spite of what it may cost. It is the courage to speak the truth into the ears of others. The word is also used in Mark 8:32; John 7:4, 13, 26, 10:24; 11:14; 2 Corinthians 3:12; 7:4; Ephesians 3:12; 6:19; Philippians 1:20.

We need to accept the fact that we are not going to make everyone happy by sharing God's good news but we are imparting truth that can save them. When Peter spoke on the Day of Pentecost the listeners were people from all across the Roman empire and they were deeply moved with sorrow and agitation as a result of what he said. This sorrow and agitation came about over the realisation that it was their sins that crucified Jesus the Messiah. Their response was, "What must we do to be saved?" The answer is to repent or change your minds and direction of your lives back towards God in order to be cleansed and forgiven for sins and immersed in the Name of Lord Yahweh, Yeshua. Peter is saying that Lord Yahweh and Jesus are one and the same. Once the people repent and are immersed in water, they will receive the gift of the Holy Spirit to empower them to live in union with Christ and other believers. Acts 2:36-41.

Peter links repentance to having our sins removed as we turn back towards God and are baptised in the Name of Jesus, the Anointed One. He then goes on to draw attention to the fact that the outpouring of the Holy Spirit on the Day of Pentecost was for all the people as well as the believers, it was for Jews, Gentiles and their families. It was for everyone whom the Lord our God was calling to Himself from all across the nations. The Church being birthed into life on the Day of Pentecost was a mixture of Jews and Gentiles coming into repentance before God. This is because it was both Jews and Gentiles who were jointly responsible for crucifying the Lord Jesus. He died for all of our sins and each one must take personal responsibility before God for causing the death of Jesus as a result of our sins. Without this willingness we cannot be saved. God would have us full of deep sorrow and intense emotional agitation for the sins we have committed that put Jesus on the cross. As Jesus Himself said in Luke 7: 36-50, those who have been forgiven much will love much.

In Acts 3: 19 Peter is saying we must repent and turn back to God or be converted. The Greek word used here is "epistrepho" and means not only repent but return home to God's grace and truth. It is returning home to the Lord our God and Father as the lost and dead son in Jesus' parable in Luke 15: 11-32. When we do this our sins are both cancelled and obliterated. God restores us to Himself and gives us a completely new life in Christ. Praise God for His marvellous grace, mercy and unfailing love.

Genesis 3: 15 opens the door of prophetic Scripture about the Messiah followed by Deuteronomy 18: 15-19. Peter declares that every prophet from Samuel onwards prophesied about the Messiah in some way. The Torah or Old Testament gives us a gradual portrait of the Messiah's suffering, death, glorification and return. Isaiah 53. Everything gradually revealed in the Old Testament points to the Messiah's promised coming in human form, death by crucifixion, resurrection followed by the coming Day of the Lord, when He returns to rule the nations in power and glory.

In Acts 3: 21, Peter declares that the Messiah will restore universally. He uses the Greek word "apokatastasis" meaning the restoration of creation to the state of existence before the Fall, alongside the restoration of the Davidic Covenant. It is also a medical term meaning "restoration of perfect health". The work of the cross begins the restoration of Paradise within the hearts of Christ's followers. "And let us run with endurance the race God has set before us. We do this by keeping our eyes on Jesus, the champion who initiates and perfects our faith. Because of the joy awaiting Him, He endured the cross, disregarding its shame. Now He is seated in the place of honour beside God's throne.

Think of all the hostility He endured from sinful people, then you won't become weary and give up". Hebrews 12: 2-3 NLT.

To know and experience God's life through Jesus Christ we must surrender to Him and let Him come in through invitation. When we open our eyes, light comes in. When we open our lungs, air comes in. When we open our hearts to Christ, He comes in to live in us forever. Although He is the Creator of the universe, He will never force His way in, as He never violates our freedom to choose. Right now, He is standing at the doorway to your heart and waiting for you to open the door to invite Him in. There is only one handle on the hearts door and it is on the inside, it must be opened by us from the inside to invite Christ in and when we do, He will come. Revelation 3: 20.

This is the meaning of Jesus' crucifixion, it occurred for us all to make living relationship with God possible through the sacrificial death of the sinless Son of God for each one of us to reconcile us back towards God. Jesus took our place on the cross, He died for our sins so that we can now be forgiven and made righteous or right with God. His atonement is an eternal, timeless sacrifice applicable to all mankind, in every generation. Amazing love how can it be, that thou my God should die for me? In the Book of Acts the jailer asks Paul, "what must I do to be saved?". Paul's answer in chapter 16 is to believe and receive and when he did, he was saved along with all of his immediate family when they also believed and received. This was the beginning of a new Church family in the Roman colony of Philippi. Acts 16: 23-40. Church family in Philippi began with the conversion of a business woman, a demonized slave girl and a jailer and his family. Only God can bring so many different people together to worship and serve Him and His Kingdom in this world.

In Acts 16: 16-22 we are introduced to the python spirit which is an evil spirit entering human lives to constrict and control them. In Parkhead some years ago we had an encounter with this spirit, when a young woman came into our healing room for prayer from the streets. She sat down in front of us and was unable to speak or communicate as she sat a whole bag of medication down beside her on the floor. In the Spirit we saw this huge snake demon wrapped around her body with its tail going down her throat and when she allowed us to break its power and deliver her, she began to speak and praise God. She came back to see us the following week totally transformed and free from all medication as she had flushed it all down the toilet pan. Like the young woman in the Acts story, she had been delivered and set free by wonderful Jesus and the power of the Holy Spirit.

I am writing to you about this just to give you one example of the timeless truth of Jesus and the holy Bible. Every one of us needs to move in the gift of discernment in these last days to recognise and deliver people crushed and constricted. God is arming us to be His open gates and doors of destiny in Psalm 24 and He is coming through us like a mighty, victorious warrior to win the battle for the souls of men. The world and all the people in it belong to God and He is the rightful Owner and Creator, He is coming to save and restore and deliver everything and everyone back to Himself. Just as He pushed back the oceans, He is pushing back the works of the enemy through His living gateways and ageless doors of destiny. Welcome the King of Glory for He is about to come through you! God is wakening us up and flinging wide our doors because He is ready for battle and armed and He is looking for a Church ready to let Him come through. He is the Mighty One, invincible in battle and Commander of the army angels in heaven and they are being released and commissioned to serve His end times plans and purposes alongside His Bride the victorious Church.

I encourage you reader to invite Christ into your life so that you are forgiven and born anew into His eternal family and so that you can spend the rest of your life serving His destiny plans for your life. In His great wisdom, God has chosen men to be His ambassadors by going outside the walls of the Church to share His Good News, for it is the only way by which people can be saved.

8

G'S STORY

H i, my name is G. Before I got saved and went to a drug rehabilitation unit my life was bad, really bad. I was locked away in darkness using drugs as well as being on a methadone programme. I remember sitting and thinking to myself, how did things get to this stage? Am I a jinx or cursed or something?

As far back as I can remember when I was just a young boy of four, I was troubled with sexual, physical and mental abuse, which shattered my confidence. I hated school because I was dyslexic and the teachers isolated me in a corner every day and this led to me being name called and bullied. As I got older, I started taking heavier drugs. At 15 I became involved in the dance scene and hanging out with older guys and this led to acts of violence, drug dealing and drug taking. I used to stop and think from time to time that this was not the plan for me, there must be more to life than this.

This went on for years until I became really broken and found myself sitting in a dingy old flat in the darkness and I didn't come out for eleven years. People would try to communicate with me through my letter box. I had hourly thoughts of suicide going through my head as I could see no light at the end of the tunnel. I heard a quiet voice telling me to go to a nearby church, which turned out to be a wake- up call and a lifeline for me. The leaders of the church invited me to an Alpha course and church meetings on the Sunday and I managed to go for six weeks. They also helped and supported me to reduce my drug intake and eventually I was able to apply for rehabilitation.

I gave up my house, dog and possessions and went into the rehab centre where I began a journey adjusting to rules, regulations and good discipline. The programme was difficult at first but God gave me the grace to continue and accept trying times because of my own issues and others around me. My life had been a real mess for many, many years through drug taking and other things but gradually God began to speak to me and show me that He had a wonderful plan for my life.

Jesus has been faithful in revealing His purposes to me and blessing me with new health, life without drugs and the desire to serve Him by helping others who are addicted. I met my beautiful wife just months ago when she also found herself in rehab and God clearly led us together to become a powerful partnership to spread the Kingdom of God, everywhere we go. She is the perfect partner for me because she has been through many of the same issues and God brought us together for one another and to help others trapped in lives of addiction. Recently we both started volunteering and this has led to us getting some paid work with people from a similar background to us still trapped in addiction. I love to sit down with marginalised people, share my story with them and show them that if God can change me, He can change anybody. I used to think I had no qualifications but how wrong I was because my life gave me everything needed to help others through my experiences and trials. I love reaching out to homeless and marginalised people on the city streets to show them there is hope because Jesus loves them. How I thank God for the change He made in me in less than one year of rehabilitation at the rehab centre and He can and will do the same for you if you give Him the chance to do so. Glory be to Jesus for giving me new life and hope. I recently achieved my SVQ 3 in Social Care not bad for a boy written off at school and I give God all the glory for it.

Then you will know the truth, and the truth will set you free. John 8:32.

Permission given by G for his story.

9

SAVED FROM SUICIDE

Recently, we found ourselves down by the river next to the suspension bridge speaking to a man who looked desperate for help. Some months before he had tried to commit suicide by throwing himself off the bridge but had been rescued before the noose, he had used had taken his full weight. He was admitted to hospital in a coma, which lasted some months and his wife thought he was going to die so she tragically committed suicide and he felt great guilt and shame over what had happened. He had gone there to commit suicide that day, blaming himself for the circumstances of his wife's death. He listened as we told him how precious to God both he and his wife were. He told us he could see his wife beckoning him to come and dance with her on the surface of the water but our prayers prevailed and he allowed us to take him away to the city mission to a place of safety. He allowed us to keep in touch as we saw him safely home in a taxi that day from the banks of the river. I visited him days later and he thanked us so much for intervening to help him. It was great to be able to pray with him and further assure him of God's continuing love for him as he works through the difficulties of his past. As we sat listening to him, we were so aware of the fact that he did not know his true identity as a son of God and lacked real meaning and purpose in his life and this is so true of so many today, which is why many try to end their lives in so many tragic ways.

As human beings made in the image and likeness of God, we are designed to know who we are and why we are here. We were designed to live by faith in our creator God through a relationship based on His love for us. When faith is used the supernatural and the miraculous follow because the life of Christ is released deep inside and the resting place of His love becomes the root and source of our lives. Every life requires a root and source to discover and experience meaning, purpose and fulfilment. Our root and source are the love Christ and the Father has for each one of us made uniquely in His likeness to fulfil His plans and purposes.

We are simply here to learn by faith to rest in Christ's extravagant, astonishing love for us. This is a journey of discovery and experience as we learn how deeply intimate and far reaching His love is. It transcends understanding, as it pours in, filling us to overflowing with the fullness of God. Yes, God wants everyone of His children to be filled to overflowing with His fullness. What could be more wonderful and satisfying than this? We were made to experience this love as it reveals who we are and why we are here. This is Apostle Paul's prayer for us in Ephesians 3: 14-21 TPT.

It is a passionate prayer for a people passionately loved with an eternal destiny in Christ. It is a prayer revealing God has more to reveal during both time and eternity. There is so much more that time is too short and eternity necessary. As we discover and experience Christ's love and transformed by its power, we are empowered to love as He loves. His love becomes a river of life and power within, liberating our whole beings to love using the supernatural resources of heaven made available and accessible to us. I personally think this to be the greatest prayer in the Bible. Why don't you use it as a template or pattern to pray over your own life and others? It is a prayer of five separate parts, which God will always answer because it is written in Scripture for all time and eternity. It is five prayers gathered together into one as seen from the perspective of verse breaks in 14-16, 17, 18-19, 20, 21. It is a revelation, which unveils Christ's love for us to empower us to love as He loves. If you choose to use these prayers in your devotional life, you will experience transformation inside and out and they will equip you to be able to pray powerfully and with authority for others. See if you can discover at least nine different aspects of Christ's love and look deeper into each using word searches and dictionary definitions. If you have been asking God to teach you how and what to pray here is one of the answers, written forever for you in the Scriptures as a great pattern to be followed. Our daily walk with God is a mixture of discovery, experience and knowledge as He reveals who He is and who we are and why we are here. These are important questions to have answered for all of us. They provide us with the Father's love and security, He intended we enjoy in this life.

I now want to look at one of Jesus' parables in Matthew 22: 1-14 titled the parable of the great feast. In this story the guests invited to attend are those responding to God's invitation by repentance and faith in the way of the cross.

The King spots a man clothed in different garments and asks him why he was there because he was improperly dressed. "Friend, how is it that you are here without wedding clothes?" The man is speechless as he is put out of the banquet and thrown into outer darkness to experience regret and loss. Many hear the call of grace but few in comparison respond and receive His wedding garments but none the less the banquet hall is filled with wedding guests. You are being invited to the King's great wedding feast for His Son right now. His banquet is nearly ready and He wants to know if you are coming. He has sent His servants out to you many times throughout your life to tell you everything as God sends His servants out to invite many but they refuse to come on His terms, the terms of grace. Eventually the banquet hall is full and ready and this is the day of your salvation. You have no wedding clothes of your own good enough for the occasion but the King is supplying you with the best robe in His house the robe of His righteousness dipped in the sinless blood of Jesus, His Son crucified for you. You can come today, washed, graced, restored and delivered in Jesus' Name. Are you ready to come right now?

In John 3 and 4 we see two very different people being invited to the King's wedding banquet. In John 3: 1-16 we see Nicodemus whose name means Conqueror coming to Jesus and he was a distinguished, good moral man. In John 4 it is an immoral woman coming to Jesus. The woman's name was Photini and Jewish historians tell us she went on to become a great evangelist who led firstly her family to Christ, her whole village and ended up leading one of Nero's daughters to Christ in Rome, where she died for her faith. The living water of the Holy Spirit given to her by Jesus transformed her life and many others as it flowed through her.

Jesus tells Nicodemus that the spiritual realm gives birth to the supernatural life he is searching for and thirsting for. The water of the Word of God cleanses and gives us new life. In the beginning of God's creation, the Holy Spirit hovered over the chaotic waters Genesis 1: 1-2, and new creation life comes the same way as Holy Spirit hovers over us then gives birth to our spirits. We are born of water and Spirit-wind to enter God's Kingdom realm. The wind, the breath and the Spirit are moved by mysterious moods and in their own wonderful ways. When we feel their touch and hear their voices, we know they are real but we don't understand how they flow and move over the earth. In this same mysterious way so is everyone who is born by wind, breath and Spirit. In the realm of the Spirit, heaven and earth are one and only those seated in the heavenly realms in Christ can understand spiritual truths. 1 Corinthians 2: 1-10. Nicodemus became a conqueror in Christ as he experienced the Holy Spirit for himself as we all must do.

Thank God for this man, the first of five men all saved from taking their own lives down at the Clyde Walkway in 2019. On average two people go there every week to attempt suicide, so please pray that we would be in the right place at the right time to intervene and help them. If you can find the time to walk the area and release the healing, saving presence of God that would be marvellous. Praise God for the victory we have through Jesus Christ our Lord.

10

FEAR GOD AND LIVE

This is the question asked by the criminal on the cross beside Jesus as the other criminal chastised Jesus rather than repenting before Him. Luke 23: 40. God's word tells us that we are all under the death sentence of sin. Romans 3: 23 and 6: 23. So what can we do about it? The answer is exactly the same thing as this criminal did when he acknowledged Jesus as a King with a coming Kingdom and repented before Him. You see we have all been sentenced to die both physically and spiritually without hope in Christ. Our death sentence can only be revoked through the exchange of Christ for us on the cross. The criminal acknowledges that Jesus had done nothing wrong, He was suffering for our sins not His and the man also acknowledges that he was dying justly for the wrong things he had done. Jesus gives him and us an amazing promise, today you will be with Me in paradise. This man had no time to serve God, no time to make God love him more or less all he could do was call on Jesus for mercy and mercy he received.

The crucifixion of God in Christ is man's lowest point and most terrible crime and yet it is God's highest demonstration and revelation of His love for us. By forgiving us on the cross, Jesus opened the doors of salvation and forgiveness for everybody, everywhere, forever. He opened the floodgates of God's grace love and mercy to flow like a mighty river bursting its banks with kindness forever over mankind. Man's greatest need is to be loved and as a child of God we are loved forever with a perfect love higher than any other. A loving Father humbled Himself to become in and through His only Son, flesh, sin, and a curse for us, in order to redeem us without compromising His own character. God did not love us because Jesus died. Jesus died because God loved us. The heart of the Father is genuine love, a love that was not the result of the cross but the reason for it.

God has the same love for Israel as He has for His Church, an everlasting love which draws us to Him as it is unfailing. It is a love that is rebuilding the greatest of all the nations. God is saving His people the remnant of Israel and we must thank God for them and pray for the peace of Jerusalem. In 2 Peter 1: 19 we are told that prophecy is a light shining in a dark place so we must become familiar with every word of prophecy yet to be fulfilled in Scripture to shine Christ's light in the darkest places. Matthew 24 is called the spine of all Bible prophecy so we must study this chapter to prepare ourselves for all that is yet to come and act upon it. All Israel cannot be saved until the full number of the Gentiles comes in according to Romans 11. We must take full responsibility to preach the gospel to all the nations so that the Jews can be saved. Matthew 24: 14.

In Romans 5: 1-2 we read that faith in Jesus transfers God's righteousness to us and as a result God declares us as flawless in His eyes. What does this mean? It means we can now enjoy true and lasting union and peace with God and beginning now, we can enjoy Him forever. Faith in Jesus opens the door into the presence of God where He welcomes us as His children by clothing us with His righteous robe, the best robe in the Father's house, His own robe. God longs for a deeply intimate and far- reaching love relationship with us because He created us to know and enjoy Him forever. Religious people rarely enjoy God, this is a pleasure kept for relational people. God burns with a passionate love for the love and devotion of His children. He is complete without us but we are incomplete without Him. Faith in Jesus also opens the door to permanent access to God's marvellous kindness and grace. Standing in God's marvellous kindness and grace is experiencing a perfect relationship with Him.

It is the perfect sacrifice of the Lord Jesus Christ which makes all of this possible. God wants us to enjoy abundant peace and well-being in every area of our lives as we learn to relate to Him. How many of us believers really see ourselves as flawless in God's eyes? Grace can be a strange and foreign language to us but it is God's love language. Society mostly rewards those who work for things and deserve them, it rarely demonstrates grace. Grace tells us that all God requires of us is satisfied by the sacrifice of Jesus for us on the cross. That the Christ living in us by faith is enough to satisfy God. It tells us that in relationship with God there is nothing we can do to make Him love us more or less. This is the divine love language of grace. Through the coming ages, we will be the visible display of the infinite, limitless riches of His grace and kindness, which was showered upon us in Jesus Christ. For it was only through this wonderful grace that we believed in Him. Nothing we did could ever earn this salvation, for it was the gracious gift from God that brought us to Christ. So, no one will be able to boast, for salvation is never a reward for good works or human striving. Ephesians 2: 7-9 TPT.

In the Garden of Eden God asked the man Adam, "Where are you?" God was deliberately and intentionally pursuing Adam to confront him about sin and prevent him from eating of the tree that would have cursed him eternally with no hope of salvation. Mankind was never created to experience the death of godlessness. We are never more alive when we are completely reconciled back to God with no desire to hide from Him. People choose to hide from God behind trees of philosophy, religion and pride but just as Adam discovered, this is not possible.

Glorious freedom awaits all who will approach God on His terms of repentance, seeking His forgiveness and to be made right with Him through the cross. We discover He is a loving Father ready to accept and embrace us in tenderness and mercy. Will you come out from behind the trees, walk towards God and ask Him to save you today? You will find He is already there waiting for you. He will kiss your heart with forgiveness in spite of what you have done. Psalm 103: 1-5. The vilest offender who truly believes, that moment from Jesus a pardon receives. This was the experience of the criminal on the cross next to Jesus as He promised him that today he would be with Him in paradise.

The way into heaven is through a gate of pearl. Revelation 21: 9-27. Pearl is a product of pain. The oyster is invaded by a tiny parasite or speck of sand and its healing powers are marshalled against it at the point of peril. The oyster releases a precious secretion in order to heal the wound and save its life. The result is a pearl. A pearl is the result of a wound that has been healed. It is a reminder that the only way into heaven is through the innocent sufferings of the Messiah on the cross, who turns the cruelty of our sin and pain into a pearl. There are twelve gates into heaven and each one is a pearl.

In Matthew 13:44- 46, Jesus is speaking a parable about a pearl and treasures. He is speaking about a Person, Himself discovering pearls and treasures in a field, which is the world. See verse 38 of the same chapter as Jesus explains the parable of the sower where He teaches us that the field is the world. He is speaking about heavens kingdom realm, the realm He left to come here to look for treasures and exquisite pearls. The re-hiding of the treasure is a hint of our new life hidden with Christ in God. God's children are His treasures and rare, unique pearls exquisite in His sight. God is overjoyed to find them and sells everything He owns to exchange it all for us. Jesus left His exalted place in glory and from His wounds here on the cross comes forth His pearls, those believing in His sacrifice for them. Heavens kingdom realm was created to be filled with God's pearls and treasures, Jesus discovered us and gave His all to exchange us for the Father and Himself. It has cost Him everything He owned but out of love He came and saved us.

There are still more treasures and rare pearls to be discovered and brought into God's kingdom realm in the field of this world. We have the joy of gathering them in with the Holy Spirit as He leads us to them. We are learning to value precious soul pearls the way Jesus does. We are God's precious pearl children. Take time today to think about how much you mean to God. It cost Him everything to redeem you from the world into His kingdom. Let this truth capture your heart as you worship Him and ask Him to use you to gather other pearls and treasures in. Today I hope you and I will begin to realise how much we mean to God our Father. I also believe that Jesus was speaking about Israel in the first parable of the treasure and the Church in the second of the exquisite pearls. The pearls are just one part of the bigger treasure, which are saved Jews and Gentiles together as one Body the Church of the Living God. As the pearls we have been grafted into the bigger treasure chest of Israel the true Church of God. In Philippians 2: 6-11, Paul tells us how much it cost the Messiah to leave His Kingdom realm, come down to earth as a Man and pay the price for His pearls and treasures, it cost Him everything as He gives all He owns in exchange for us. This is exactly how much you and I mean to God because He paid everything in exchange for us to become His sons, priests and kings. Revelation 5: 10-12.

We are God's flawless sons and daughters, anointed in this world with royal favour to carry out our Father's business through priestly intercession and royal representation among the nations. When we begin to see ourselves as Father has made us in Christ, we will be an invincible army sweeping across the nations, fulfilling the great commission and ushering in the last days promise for all Israel to be saved. The next revival will be one revealing the glory of God among the nations and it will come in waves releasing such supernatural power and authority that the greatest harvest of souls ever experienced will come into the Kingdom of God. We are living in the most exciting time because God is preparing us to gather in Christ's harvest and experience something of the joy it will bring to His heart. The Father promised this to the Son in Isaiah 53 at the end of the chapter and we see a picture of it in Revelation as Jesus takes His sickle across the nations firstly for revival and reaping, then for judgement. Revelation 14: 14-20.

According to Colossians 3: 1-4 our death by sharing Christ's crucifixion to this world also releases His resurrection life into us. We cannot experience the resurrection without the crucifixion, death comes before life in the Kingdom realm. As we learn to fill our thoughts with heavenly realities something amazing is promised, we will see the revelation of who we really are in Christ and the world will also see it. This is Church resurrected with heavenly realities and walking in glorious end times revelation impacting society at the deepest levels. We live in a world devoid of heavenly realities until the Church is manifesting them openly and consistently. We are one with Him in glory, which means His glory needs to be revealed through us. This is the nature of the revival I am talking about above. We are being prepared and aligned with the crucifixion of Christ to experience His resurrection and reveal the glory of God to the nations.

We need to become a people full of the revelation of heavenly realities experiencing them ourselves and carrying them out to the nations. When we begin to live as one with Him in His glory the greatest ever harvest of souls will be reaped from among the nations. Christians are the only people on earth called to live as people who have died. To live as people who have severed the tie to this life to discover our hidden lives with Christ in God. We are really called to be a people dead to this natural realm and alive to heavenly realities to such an extent that these realities are flowing through us like a river flooding its banks with kindness, like the river of healing in Ezekiel 47: 1-12.

We have just experienced a miracle in the life of one of the street people. He came into Street Connect some time ago, needing God to heal his right leg or he was going to have it amputated two days later. Understandably he was really upset and desperate to experience God's healing power so we prayed together and although he felt nothing as we prayed when he went to the hospital two days later, he told us the doctors were dumbfounded as they discovered his leg was completely normal without need for any surgery. He was able to testify to them that he had received healing prayer for the leg just two days previously. What a wonderful testimony this is to the love and power of our God if only we will step into the river of healing faith, He promises to us. I remember praying with John on that night with Maciej and inwardly crying out for Him to heal because he was so upset and desperate for a miracle and I am glad to report that Mighty God turned up to do what He does best. I want to give God all the glory for this miracle because it could only be Him and much more is about to follow.

In Luke 2:49 Jesus asks us another question. Did you not know that I must be about My Father's business? Another version asks, didn't you realise that I should be involved with My Father's affairs? What is the Father's business and affairs? It is making it possible for lost sinners to be reconciled to Himself. Jesus came to seek out and give life to those who are lost. Luke 19: 10. The Father's business was to unveil the glorious splendour of His Son on the cross, by the empty tomb, through His ascension into heaven, and by the mighty outpouring of the Holy Spirit upon His Church. Jesus came to give us the rich knowledge and experience of eternal life by faithfully doing everything the Father asked Him to do. John 17: 1-4. He came to reveal the true nature of the Father to us so we could fully believe in Him. He came to birth a new humanity, which would belong to God and to empower us to reveal His glory to the world. He came to establish a new humanity, which would live lives pleasing to the Father and fulfil His kingdom desires and designs on earth as it is in heaven. As His disciples we are to influence the systems of this world with kingdom influences in order to transform and turn it the right way up again. Jesus came to make God more real to us and share the rich experience of the Father's endless love because it is exactly the same love Father has for Him. As Jesus lives in us by His Spirit, so the Father's endless love lives in us.

The Father's business was for Jesus, His Son, to come to this earth clothed in a human body, to offer Himself as a complete and perfect sacrifice for us, to make us right with God. By God's will we have been purified and made holy once and for all through the sacrifice of the body of Jesus, the Messiah. Hebrews 10: 10. How marvellous and wonderful is the love of Jesus and the Father for us. Romans 5: 8. Jesus is living proof of God's passionate, endless love for us. He died in our place to give us eternal life. He has satisfied God's justice on our behalf with His perfect, sinless, spotless, flawless, Lamb of God, Passover sacrifice. Exodus 12: 1-10.

There is mystery here in that our search for Him is compelled by His for us, for He is the Good Shepherd leaving the ninety- nine to search for His one lost sheep to bring it home again. Our choosing of Him is compelled by His choosing of us, that we should go and produce fruit that will last eternally. John 15: 16. The Father's affairs and business are mysterious in the sense that they are Holy Spirit revealed and directed according to His designs, patterns and perfect knowledge of all things pertaining to life and godliness. Everything comes out of God, is sustained by God and finds fulfilment in Him. May all praise and honour be given to Him forever! Amen Romans 11: 36.

Praise God for our Saviour Jesus who knew when He would die, where He would die, and how He would die. Despite this knowledge He kept moving towards His death because He also knew that without it, we would never have life. John 10: 11 tells us He is the Good Shepherd which in Greek means He is beautiful, virtuous, excellent and genuine. He is also our Great Shepherd and Shepherd King. Hebrews 13: 20 and 1 Peter 5: 4.

— 11 —

THE GOD WHO SEES YOU

The God who sees you. In Genesis 16 we have one of God's angels asking two questions as Hagar flees from her mistress Sarah. Where have you come from and where are you going? This could also be, where have you been brought from and where are you going? Never forget where you have been brought from, a life of sin, disobedience and separation from God. We have been brought from a godless life and eternity into a godly life and destiny. God has brought us out of darkness into His glorious light, so we can fulfil our destiny. Where are we going? Hopefully forwards into all God has planned for us as individuals and as a community or Church.

God sees us, cares about us and loves us, which is why He wants us to see that He sees us. You matter to God because He came to save and redeem you for Himself and His plans and purposes. God is El Rohe the God who sees you, as He guides you as your Shepherd King. When you begin to see that God sees you as important, then your life will change forever, as you will then believe in and more deeply experience, His endless love for you. Never think that you do not matter to God because He knows everything about you in the most intimate detail and He loves you. In Psalm 139 the Holy Spirit makes these truths abundantly clear to us. You are here right now because God planned for you and has plans for you. You are very, very precious to God and His purposes for mankind.

No two people have the same finger print even though our planet contains over seven billion people. Don't you find this remarkable? In the same way God has a unique plan for every human life. We each have a completely unique identity in Christ to follow and develop here on earth. Hagar was unique, which is why God asked her to remember where she had been brought from and where she was going. When we remember where we have been brought from, we can better grasp where we are going. We can never go back into the world and be content and happy after being chosen by God. John 15: 16. God has chosen us to experience a loving relationship with Him through which He chooses to reveal His destiny plans for our lives. We must move forwards into God revealed destiny just as Hagar and Ishmael, even if moving forwards means pain and rejection.

People may misunderstand or reject you in your pursuit of God given destiny but you must hold onto it just as Jesus had to throughout His life here on earth. Jesus' destiny was to go right on through to the cross to pay the penalty for our sins and salvation and make us right with God. Even those closest to Him failed to see this and even tried to prevent Him from achieving it. The disciple Peter in particular tried to divert Jesus from His goal to the point where Jesus had to rebuke him. The people around Jesus enjoyed His miracles and teaching but still failed to understand the true nature of His destiny and calling. Jesus knew where He had been brought from and where He was going. He had been brought from heaven to earth to live a sinless life as Son of Man, be filled with God's Spirit, to save mankind through the sacrifice of the cross. Jesus knew where He was going, to the cross. He knew He was called by God to defeat sin, evil and Satan on the cross. He knew where He was going and why, and He went with determination and willingness, under the grace of God.

Just imagine if like Jesus, you knew where you would die, when you would die and how. Even though Jesus knew all of this, He remained steadfast to God's destiny plan in order to save us. This shows us how much He loves us. Romans 5: 8. Jesus did not deserve to die and we did not deserve to live but God so loved the world that He gave His only begotten Son, so that everyone believing in Him shall live forever. John 3: 16, 17. Jesus was driven by love to fulfil God's destiny plan for Him and us, despite the terrible physical, mental and spiritual pain involved. Thank God for Jesus' far- reaching love for us in spite of all we have done. He could have gone back to heaven at any time without the cross but chose not to out of love and concern for all of us. My dear reader can I ask you, where have you been brought from and where are you going? Have you been reconciled to God through the precious blood of Jesus the sinless, Lamb of God? If you surrender your own life to God, He will show you His plans for your new life in Christ. It is only as we learn to lay down our lives that we can find true life in Christ. Unless a seed falls down to the ground and dies it remains alone but when it dies it produces a harvest. John 5.

Hagar was running away when God saw her and perhaps you also have been running from God and His plans for your life. Hagar was given a promise by God if only she would submit, return and serve for a little longer. She would multiply and bear much fruit for her humility and obedience to God. Hagar was forced to make a very costly personal decision not just for herself but also for her son Ishmael. Would she choose God's way or her own? She had to remember where she had been brought from and where she was going. The God who had seen her had revealed a wonderful plan for her life and He also has a wonderful plan for yours. God sees you.

When the woman at the well came to fetch water at the hottest part of the day, God could see her. She came when she thought the well would be deserted but God was there waiting for her. This encounter with Jesus at the well would change her life forever, she would never be the same woman again afterwards. She changed because she took a drink which became a river within her. Read John 4 and John 7: 37-39. Only Jesus promises to satisfy our spiritual thirst for God and His Kingdom realm. When we only drink of the water of this world, we are going to be thirsty once again because it is not living water. Rivers of living water will burst out from within us, flowing out from Christ's throne within, as a drink becomes a river. Jewish history tells us that

Photini, the woman at the well in John 4 experienced this after her encounter with Jesus. This was a very personal encounter, something we all need to experience with Him. As she drank Christ's living water it became a river within flowing out to her family and community, where she turned many to Christ, so they could also come and drink. The river within took her all the way into the courts of Nero the Roman emperor, where she led one of his daughters to Christ and was martyred for it. Photini took a drink and became a river of living water and by so doing she fulfilled God's destiny plan for her life, as she impacted others around her for the Kingdom of God. Will you come to Jesus and drink to become a river of living water?

The cross was an expected event and not an afterthought. Jesus is the Lamb slaughtered and slain from before the creation of the world. Revelation 13: 8. In Isaiah 52: 13 God says He is going to cleanse many nations and we need to pray that the United Kingdom would be one of those nations that are cleansed by God. Then it goes on to say that many kings will stand speechless in God's presence as they see and understand the Gospel. Those in authority need to see and understand before Almighty God and we are asked to pray for them and must take our responsibility more seriously. In Isaiah 53 we are told that the Messiah carried our sicknesses and diseases, was pierced for our rebellion, crushed for our sins and beaten so that we could be healed. Because we have left God's paths to follow our own all our iniquities, transgressions and sins were laid on Him.

Jesus has many spiritual descendants or seed as a result of His obedience at the cross. He will see and be satisfied by all that is accomplished through His sufferings. Many will be counted righteous as a result of Him bearing all their sins. On the cross, Christ paid the full price for all of our sins so that we can now be whole and healed spiritually, mentally and physically. We can be blessed with every spiritual blessing in the heavenly realms through our union with Him and there are no infirmities in the heavenly realms, only wholeness and life. Even before He created the world God loved us and chose us to be holy and without fault in His eyes. God's children bring Him great pleasure as we live in obedience to Him in this realm. Our freedom has been purchased with the blood of God's Son and all our sins forgiven. He has showered His kindness upon us along with all wisdom and understanding. Everything in heaven and earth will be brought together under the authority of Jesus Christ. Ephesians 1: 1-10. Sin, sickness, disease, infirmity will be no more under Christ's authority. God's salvation is spirit, soul and body because like Him we are created as triune in essence and all three parts of our essence requires salvation. This is the Good News preached in the power of the Holy Spirit sent from heaven. It is so powerful that even angels are watching eagerly for God's prophetic words to be fulfilled in all the nations. 1 Peter 1: 10-12.

Peter is saying that more unveiling of Christ is occurring in these last days as predicted by God's prophets Enoch, Abraham, Jacob, Moses, Elijah, Elisha, Isaiah and Jeremiah. The Spirit of Christ rested on each one of these Old Covenant prophets as they understood their predictions were not for their time but for generations to come. Jesus is being unveiled or revealed to His Church and the world in a more complete way during these last days so that His people can stand strong in His mighty power throughout all our difficulties and persecutions. We await a glorification that cannot be described as God continually watches over and protects us. Christ is ready to be revealed and waits for our discovery.

True salvation demands a response, a sacrificial response. The cross and Jesus' resurrection need to change us if we are going to change the world. Beloved friends, what should be our response to God's marvellous mercies? This is Paul's question in Romans 12: 1,2. To respond involves surrender and sacrifice. It involves living in holiness to experience all that delights God's heart. A response like this is a genuine expression of worship. Present day culture presents ideals and opinions contrary to the Word of God in order to try and squeeze us into its mould but we must resist this at all costs. Rather we must imitate Christ as He lives within transforming us from the inside out beginning with our thinking. Our thinking must be continually moulded by the Word of God so that our living is dynamically changed after the pattern of Christ.

Can we live enthusiastically for God with a boiling hot passion for Him? Can we radiate with the glow of the Holy Spirit, allowing Him to fill us with excitement as we serve Him? Holy Spirit is transforming us into a people who are loving, haters of evil, devoted, loyal, enthusiastic, joyful and persistent. If we commune with God at all times, we will speak blessing, not cursing, over those who reject and persecute us. God would have us live humble lives at peace with other people. We have the power to defeat evil with goodness as we walk in the favour of our God. All of these virtues involve surrender and sacrifice, which delight God's heart and are genuine expressions of worship.

Jesus speaks about trees and houses in Luke 6: 43-49. The trees produce either good or bad fruit and the houses stand or fall according to their foundations. What kind of fruit are we producing and where are we choosing to place our foundations? How can we say Christ is our Lord, Master and Owner if we do not put His teachings into practice? Christ's teachings are deep and secure and will keep us standing strong when the inevitable storms come but we must be confident about this or we may well waver in the face of the storm. A tree will bend and give during a storm because its roots are deeply planted into the bedrock below. Each one of us chooses where we build our house-character and where we choose to plant our roots to produce fruit. My child, pay attention to what I say. Listen carefully to My words. Don't lose sight of them. Let them penetrate deep into your heart, for they bring life to those who find them, and healing to their whole body. Guard your heart above all else, for it determines the course of your life. Proverbs 4: 20-22 NLT.

We must arise and join Jesus outside the religious walls seeking to restrain us. We must follow Christ's example by showing mercy to others by doing acts of kindness to help them for these things delight God's heart. God wants to activate His Gospel message both inside and outside the walls of Church so that it changes us and the world we live in. James or Jacob as his true Hebrew name would be asks us questions. My dear brothers and sisters, what good is it if someone claims to have faith but demonstrates no good works to prove it? How could this kind of faith save anyone? Faith that doesn't involve action is dead, fruitless, false and phony. God's gift of righteousness is seen clearly in us by our faith expressed through our actions. For just as a human body without the spirit is a dead corpse, so faith without the expression of good works is dead. James 2: 14-26 TPT.

People claiming to be Christians, who fail to surrender and sacrifice to the teachings of Christ in the Bible and do not follow the impulses of the Holy Spirit, are deceived and deceivers, whom we must pray for and warn fervently. There are many people like this today, who choose to selectively believe in parts of the Bible but not all of the parts, and by doing so are grieving the Holy Spirit. All Scripture is inspired by God not just some. 2 Timothy 3: 16-17. The same Scriptures warn us about the last days, days we are now living in since Pentecost, so we must become fervent believers of all Scripture and guard against all forms of false and deceptive teaching, which usually eliminates the gifts and anointings of the Holy Spirit.

For anyone to feel they have little need for the ministry anointings and giftings of the Holy Spirit today is madness because without Holy Spirit we can do nothing significant with God. To relegate the Holy Spirit as a bystander is following a gospel of works and the flesh, which is a false gospel. They are people who follow a form of religion but deny its power. This is no good to anybody at all except the devil who continually strives to hold them in bondage to it. God's heart is breaking for them and so should ours.

When Christ declared, "It is finished" from the cross, He was saying that His mightiest work was accomplished there. What was that work? It was the work of revelation, redemption and reconciliation. The self-revelation of God, the atonement for sin, and the opening of a way whereby a repentant, sinful humanity could enter once more into the presence of a holy God. In Greek Jesus said Tetelestai, or it has been and will for ever remain finished. On the cross, Jesus paid our sin debts bills in full and we must stand in awe at God's goodness and love demonstrated for us at Calvary.

How can we stand with God in these last days and not be moved as gradually a global culture arises, which will war against God's people and God Himself? A great apostasy or falling away is predicted to occur at the end of the age as a godless world culture seeks to merge all others into one and compel everyone to abandon their faith. Any culture, faith, people or person that stands in its way, it will eradicate. We need to be ready to face a global culture that persecutes God's people, abolishes God's Word, blasphemes God's Names and desecrates the sacred things of God. There are many signs that this Abomination is fast approaching like an unstoppable train.

Are we prepared to stand strong in the Lord and in His mighty power? Are we ready to go against the flow, fight the fight and light up the coming darkness? Isaiah 60: 1-2. Jesus, the greatest of all the prophets, speaks about these things in Matthew chapters 24 and 25. In these chapters Jesus is foretelling the future. He has been walking in the Temple grounds in Jerusalem with His disciples, who are attracted by the beautiful ornamental buildings and tells them they are all going to be destroyed. The disciples respond by asking Him two questions. Tell us when will all this happen? What sign will signal Your return and the end of the age? TPT asks what supernatural sign should we expect to signal Your coming and the end of the age? Jesus begins His answers by addressing the second question and He introduces the fact that many signs will lead up to one main sign. The signs are deception, revolutions, wars, earthquakes, epidemics and famines. Matthew 24: 1-8. Throughout this time believers will be persecuted and a great falling away or apostasy will occur as a result of much false prophecy. As believers we must endure this season to experience life and deliverance.

In Matthew 24: 14, Jesus now states the main sign which is the continuing preaching of the gospel across all nations until the full number of Jews and Gentiles are saved. Romans 11: 25-27. It is because of His love for us that God will shorten this time of great suffering and persecution. Our true Messiah will appear as a sign in the sky with His mighty warriors, great splendour and glory. Angels will be sent out to gather believers from every nation from one end to another. We must continue to observe and pray for Israel, the fig tree. Jesus is coming in an hour least expected so we must continue to be faithful and gospel centred. Why observe, Israel? The devil usually attacks Israel first then the rest of the nations. Terrorism began in Israel, now it is worldwide.

Jesus continues His teaching in chapter 25 through the parables of the ten virgins, financial stewardship and judgement of the multitudes. The oil required by the Church is the Holy Spirit, filling us continually to be ready and alert for all that is coming. Jesus is looking for loyalty and faithfulness from us as we take what He gave His life for and present it, the gospel to the nations to multiply a return. When He takes His judgement seat as all the nations are gathered before Him a great separation will occur. Only those who have personally repented and responded obediently to His gospel message and reached out to others in need will be saved. By caring for the least important of humanity, we are demonstrating a genuine love for Jesus our Lord and Master by following in His footsteps. Jesus is concerned for people who happen to be hungry, thirsty, homeless and suffering the injustice of poverty and ill health. His concerns must become ours as we travel the road together as His true disciples.

Compassion, love, tenderness and caring have high priority in the Kingdom of God. I am confident that if we remain sensitive to the Holy Spirit and God's written word, we will not miss the signs and endure until the final sign is completed. When we as Church community have preached the gospel in all the nations the end of this present age will come. We are looking to Him, as He looks to us, so that together we can fulfil Scripture and trigger the end of the age.

12

HOLY SPIRIT

A cts 19:2 Did you receive the Holy Spirit when you believed? I did yes but not the fullness of the Spirit, that is an ongoing process I believe. We are to be continually filled with the Spirit according to Paul in Ephesians 4. There are two groups of twelve, the twelve at Ephesus without the Holy Spirit and the twelve apostles turning the world upside down full of the Holy Spirit. Which group of twelve are you in? Did you receive the Holy Spirit when you believed? The twelve believers at Ephesus were barely holding on and achieving very little until they had an encounter with the Holy Spirit through the apostle Paul. Each of us needs a similar encounter on a daily basis as we get to know the intimate friendship of the Holy Spirit. Surely when somebody who is God comes to live inside of us as a friend never to leave, it is possible to know them intimately. Many of us are living just like the twelve at Ephesus rather than the twelve full of the Holy Spirit, so how can we change our attitudes towards the Holy Spirit?

Jesus promised dynamic power coming upon us when the Holy Spirit comes to fill us to be His witnesses or martyrs. The word witness can also mean martyr and partner. Acts 1: 8. Gods original pattern for us is always discovered in the Scriptures and this we must seek and follow. This pattern is the original pattern for Church and it is only as we return to this pattern, can we show people on earth what God is really like. A Holy Spiritless Church does nothing for anyone and nothing for the world. Are we as open to the energising and empowering ministry of the Spirit as were our brothers and sisters of the first century because the Holy Spirit has not changed but perhaps our expectation has? Will God revive us and bring us back to where He wants us to be? Holy Spirit is Parakletos our defence attorney and the One called to stand next to us as our Helper. He comes to end the work of the curse in our lives and to save us from its every effect. He is the Redeemer who ends the curse. He is another Saviour, saving us from the power of sin, just as Jesus saves us from the guilt of sin.

Jesus makes us a promise in Acts 1: 8. He is saying that the Holy Spirit will seize us with power and empower us with His power to be His messengers, partners, martyrs and witnesses. In Acts 4: 7, Peter and John are asked another question. They had just done an act of kindness to a frail, crippled man and now they were being held to account for it. When this kind of witness gets us into trouble then we are doing something right for God. Tell us by what power and authority have you done these things? The city council attempt to intimidate the apostles so the Holy Spirit simply anoints them to witness with great boldness and courage to continue preaching God's message the gospel. They were ordinary men who had come under the influence of Jesus and been filled to overflowing with the Holy Spirit. Just weeks before Peter had been without the Holy Spirit when he denied even knowing Jesus three times because he was fearful but now, he is courageous and determined to preach God's reality. Peter had been transformed like the others who had encountered the Holy Spirit on the day of Pentecost and continued to encounter Him. In these final days we all need to experience this same transformation to be bold and courageous witnesses for Jesus Christ. We need to encounter Holy Spirit in exactly the same way as our earlier brothers and sisters.

In John 5 and Acts 1: 8, Jesus is teaching us that there are in fact seven witnesses to the fact that He is the Christ, the Messiah and the Living God. The seven witnesses are Jesus Himself, John 5:25-27. His miracles, John 5: 36. John the Baptist, John 5: 32-34. The Father, John

5: 36-38. The Scriptures, John 5: 39-40. Every Believer, Acts 1: 8. The Holy Spirit, John 14: 16, 26. Number seven is God's perfect number, so God has a perfect pattern of witness to the Christ and we are one of the seven. Working together we have a perfect witness for Christ's deity and authority to the world. The miracles of Christ therefore must be an ongoing witness through His body to the world here on earth and we need to experience them now more than ever.

Jesus is asked a question in John 5: 22, Lord how is it that You will reveal Your identity to us believers and not to everyone? Jesus answers by saying that revelation is only given to those who love and obey Him and the Father and this is not true of everyone. Revelation is imparted by the Holy Spirit as we enjoy relationship with the Godhead so revelation is relational. Love and obedience to Jesus and His Words releases revelation through relationship. Relationship is described by Jesus as Jesus and the Father coming to make their home or dwelling place in us. Revelation is imparted by the Spirit of Holiness and the Spirit if Truth. When we repent and believe in Jesus and what He has done for us, we are given revelation, which saves and brings us into a new relationship with God. Through the Holy Spirit, Jesus then imparts more and more revelation to us, His lovers and obedient friends of God. The more obedient we are to Jesus the more revelation we receive because we have been trustworthy to what has been entrusted to us through faithful obedience.

Disobedience or simple disregard hinders revelation until we obey what we already understand and know of the will of God as determined in the Scriptures one of the seven witnesses. If you feel you need more revelation about your situation, check you have been completely obedient to what God has already shown you, only then can you move onwards with God. Our relationship with Jesus works through the dynamic of love and obedient devotion to Him and His Word. We also need God's grace to remain obedient to Him and we are promised a never- ending supply. Ephesians 1: 3-8. The unbeliever cannot receive grace to repent through revelation because of their unbelief. God commands all men everywhere to repent, which is the first step in receiving any revelation. This truth also applies to God's people as we must seek to keep short accounts with God through continual repentance to receive continual revelation. God is not mocked we reap what we sow and holy living always reaps revelation from God. Jesus set the pattern because His love for the Father and us took Him to the obedience of the cross, where He died in our place as the sacrifice for our sins of disobedience. Revelation comes at a cost, it is very precious and comes through love, obedience and sacrifice. Jesus paid the full price for us and set the pattern for us to follow. This is why Jesus only reveals Himself to repentant believers and not to everyone. Revelation is relational. Peter became so anointed by the Holy Spirit that even his shadow would heal the sick and demonised and people were healed and delivered by handkerchiefs and other things anointed by apostle Paul. We are a people who are His very own encircled by Him and when others enter the circle, they experience the supernatural power of God and His goodness. We are dots within a circle surrounded by God and He has us all to Himself. We are uniquely His and surrounded by His love. Titus 2: 11-14. Surrounded by God you are safe, protected, valued, loved, secure, special and unique.

We need to align and position ourselves for these same anointings by the Holy Spirit in these last of days because God is promising to pour out His Spirit on all people once again, we are still living in the days of Pentecost, which began two thousand years ago and have never ended. Joel 2: 28-32. I remember being at an all- night prayer meeting years ago when these words were read out loud and the presence of Christ completely fell and filled the room causing all to fall down in holy reverence and fear before Him, too afraid to even open our eyes. We just lay there worshipping, repenting and glad we were still alive. We need the holy fear of God to return to the Church and the nation. In Joel chapter 3 God is calling the nations to arms to judge them for the way they have treated Israel and for scattering the Jewish people all over the world. There are thousands waiting in the valley of decision still to be saved. God is preparing us for the time when the whole earth will be filled with His glory as the waters cover the sea beds, Habakkuk 2: 14. In Habakkuk chapter 3 as in Joel, we see God moving as His brilliant splendour fills the heavens and the earth is filled with His praise. He is revealing His awesome power as people fall in distress and terror. He is coming as a Warrior King to rescue His chosen people and to save His anointed ones. Habakkuk 3: 14-16, we need to pray the United Kingdom or whatever is left of it, will be graced to stand with and pray for Israel and not invade it with anything except prayer and actions of goodness and love. Zephaniah 3: 19-20. Ask God to anoint you with the Holy Spirit to receive revelation about Israel and how He wants to use you in these last days.

At this point I feel led by the Holy Spirit to share some wonderful and helpful teaching, that will help us to know how better to pray for Israel.

When praying we need to remain within the parameters of God's Word for the nations, Matthew 24:20. We need to start from the fact that God is right and pray into being what God has already said will happen. To intercede is to remind God about what He has already revealed in His Word the Bible. We need to be clear about the plans and purposes of God as revealed. 1 Chronicles 17 is an example of this.

Secondly, we need to access God with thanksgiving and praise, which is the only way into His presence. Psalm 100: 4. We can also shout or proclaim God's Words into a situation, Jeremiah 31: 7. As far as God's promises are concerned, we can shout, praise, proclaim, pray and sing them.

Thirdly, we need to identify and confess our sins to the Lord when praying for nations. We have done wrong not they. Daniel 9: 5. This is the pattern of identification.

Fourthly, identify with God's ultimate purpose which is to set apart a people for Himself both Jews and Gentiles. That Israel becomes the special people that God is after as part of His Church as God intended. Titus 2: 11-14.

Five, that God would release the Holy Spirit upon all of Israel.

Six, that God would arise and have mercy upon His chosen people again and fulfil His promises to them by covenant. Psalm 102: 13-18.

Seven, that Jerusalem would know God's peace and by so praying for Jerusalem you will prosper as God has promised you. Psalm 122: 6.

Eight, bless and be blessed, Numbers 24: 9. This is also a pattern in Scripture. It is first mentioned in Genesis 12: 1-3 and this promise still applies to both nations and individuals in relation to the Jewish people.

Nine, don't tell God what to do. Isaiah 40: 13. The restoration of Israel is God's priority at this time, since 1948 they have returned to the promised land and are now filling the earth with fruit as they continue to bud and blossom. Isaiah 27: 6. Only nations that line up with this will prosper including the United Kingdom. From the moment the UK undermined Israel the British Empire began to disintegrate, the only nation guaranteed a permanent future in Scripture is Israel. We need to pray 2 Chronicles 7: 14 for the healing of the UK and Israel as they are dependent upon one another.

Ten, don't presume on the grace of God, rather let the Holy Spirit search our hearts to reveal sin so that all barriers can be removed. Isaiah 59: 1-2.

Finally, pray for the harvest of the Gentiles to be completed, Romans 11: 25-32. Israel cannot be saved until the full number of the harvest of the Gentiles is brought into the Kingdom of God. Take the sword of the Spirit and proclaim for Israel as in Ephesians 6: 17. Use Psalm 33: 8-12, Jeremiah 31: 10, Psalm 125: 3, Psalm 129: 5-6, Psalm 17: 7-9.

To better understand God's plans and purposes for Israel and the Church in these last days read and study Romans chapters 9-11. The epistle Paul wrote to the Church in Rome was intended to give the mixed congregation of mainly Gentiles but also Messianic Jews, revelation on the route ahead and to encourage respect and unity between believing Jews and Gentiles.

An evil spirit of deception will attempt to sweep through the Church in these latter days as regards Israel and the church so we must be prepared for this and learn how and what to pray for Israel because Israel is key to understanding the last days and the different roles played by Church and Israel. The Church has not replaced Israel in the eternal plans and purposes of God, rather both have an ongoing prophetic destiny to fulfil before the return of the Messiah. The name Israel occurs over 2,500 times in the Old Testament and 79 times in the New and not once is it ever used to describe Church. The nation of Israel is the only nation redeemed as a nation for God Himself. 1 Chronicles 17: 21. In Exodus 19: 5-6 God declares His purposes for Israel, namely as His special treasure, His holy people, His Kingdom of priests. The entire revelation of God has come to us through the Jewish people, who were given the Scriptures as stewards to all other nations. Romans 3: 1-2. In Romans 9 from verse one Paul states eight truths about the features of the Jewish people, which makes them unique. They are the adoption, glory, covenants, law, priestly service, promises, patriarchs and the Messiah. Jesus is eternally and uniquely Jewish as He is the Lion of the Tribe of Judah. Revelation 5: 5.

In John 4: 22 Jesus says something amazing when He states that salvation for all mankind is of the Jews. We owe them an incredible debt we can never repay. The Jewish people are the only people whose whole history was recorded prophetically before it ever happened. The Bible records their enslavement in Egypt even as far back as Genesis 15, hundreds of years before it happened. Their deliverance is predicted and that their descendants would occupy the land of Canaan. The Temple destruction is predicted and the return of the exiles from Babylon and the captivity. The second Temple destruction is predicted by Jesus the greatest of all the prophets and this occurred in AD 70. Their scattering and persecution, is predicted alongside their regathering which has happened this century back to the land of Israel. Throughout all this time the Hebrew people refused to give up their identity, even though they were scattered amongst one hundred different nations all across the earth. Out of the nineteen major prophecies in the Bible about Israel only three remain to be fulfilled. Zechariah 12: 2-3 speaks about the nations gathering against Jerusalem and even now the UN want to make Jerusalem non-Jewish and may try to use force to do this in the near future. Arab neighbours have surrounded Jerusalem and will gather against her but they will be defeated according to the Scriptures in Zechariah 12-14. Finally, there will be a supernatural revelation of the Messiah to the Jews when He returns to the Mount of Olives when He will fight against their enemies, the oppressing nations. Zechariah 12: 10 and 14: 3-5. In Psalm 33: 8-12 we have a prophetic declaration of God against the nations who rise up against His own inheritance Israel. To summarise, there will be a gathering of all nations against Israel. It will be an initial success for these nations but then Jesus will return and utterly defeat them as He fights for His people.

In Zechariah there is a sequence of at least ten events recorded in chapters 12-14.

1. Nearby nations will attack Israel but will fail. 12: 1-3.
2. The Lord will begin to destroy those nations. 12: 9.
3. Messiah will be revealed to the Jews. 12: 10.
4. Forgiveness will come to the Jews through this revelation. 13: 1.
5. God will erase idol worship from the land of Israel and false prophecy. 13: 1-
6. Further away nations will now attack Israel in a united attack and Jerusalem will fall. 14: 1-2.
7. Jesus will return to the Mount of Olives, causing an earthquake and He will fight against all the nations gathered against Israel. 14: 1-11.
8. Jesus will send a plague on all the nations fighting against Jerusalem. 14: 12
9. Those who survive this plague and repent will come to Jerusalem to worship King Jesus. 14: 16.10. The nations refusing to worship in Jerusalem will be cursed with no rain. 14: 18.

13

P'S STORY

I have always known God was real. At the age of eleven I was born again but in my teenage years I began to fall away although I still went to church with my parents. As time went on, I stopped going because I didn't want to lose my friends.

I started smoking and drinking with my friends but my parents still managed to drag me along to Church so I began to drift further and further away by drinking a lot and going out partying at the weekends. This cycle went on for about ten years until I began to realise that I wasn't enjoying this way of life anymore. I had difficulty sleeping, I was having terrible nightmares and I was stressed and very anxious most of the time. I felt tired and desperately unhappy. It felt like walking around under a dark cloud. I questioned the point of my life and felt that if I was not here it would make no difference at all.

When my grannie passed away everything began to change. I was very close to her and had the privilege of caring for her during her final year. She was a born again Christian and I don't doubt for one second, she was praying for me. It was at her funeral that I had an encounter with the Holy Spirit. My Pastor was speaking about how this life is not all there is and that by being born again you have hope for eternal life. I felt as if my chest was going to explode as God's truth exposed me and I felt changed and really different. Over the next couple of months, I began to pray beginning with the sinner's prayer. I felt God's overwhelming peace when I said this as it flooded all over me. I felt that Jesus had filled the void in me that I had been trying to fill with everything else.

My younger brother was born again the following weekend and as he phoned to tell me, I was able to share my own experience with him. Neither of us had any clue about what God was doing in our lives and we were and are still amazed by His goodness, mercy and grace. I just knew this time that nothing was going to stop me from following Jesus as my Lord. I wanted to get baptised as soon as possible and so my brother and I were both baptised together in Loch Lomond. This was a very special day for us because our parents were baptised in Loch Lomond and my mom was pregnant with my younger brother at the time.

I am now at peace because Jesus is my Lord, which means He is sitting in the driver's seat, not me. I am so blessed, thankful and overwhelmed by God's grace, patience and love for me. God has given me this promise from Philippians 1: 6. And I am certain that God, who began the good work within you, will continue His work until it is finally finished on the day when Christ Jesus returns. P's Story is given by permission.

14

IMMANUEL PATTERN

Jesus modelled prayer as a pattern for us to follow. Being devoted to God means devotion to the sheer joy of learning to communicate daily with Him who is our loving Heavenly Father. Is it not sheer joy to develop a relationship with God? The Church was born in a prayer meeting. Let us begin this chapter by looking at Titus. Titus is encouraging us to live in this world with wisdom, righteousness and devotion to God. Titus 2: 11-15.

Titus was a Greek convert from Antioch and an apostolic church planter much like Timothy, his peer. He was likely a convert of Paul's ministry during his visit to Cyprus. Paul describes him as a true son in Titus 1: 4. Legend records Titus as a poet and student of Greek philosophy when he had a prophetic dream that led him to study the Word of God and become a Christ follower. As God's faithful servant he travelled with Paul on his third missionary journey. 2 Corinthians 2: 12-13, 7: 5-15, 8: 6-24. Paul commends him for his love, steadfast faith and for bringing comfort to God's people. After leaving Timothy in Ephesus, Paul accompanied Titus to Crete and left him there to establish the young church and set things in order. Believers, who had been in the upper room had returned to Crete Acts 2: 11, and were in need of guidance and leadership from Titus. The theme of Titus is that right living will always accompany right doctrine. If we say we follow Christ, our faith must be demonstrated by right living. God's saving grace is the same grace that empowers us to live for Him. Titus reminds us that right beliefs should impact every area of our lives such as family, relationships, work, community, personal choices and behaviour. Read through the epistle and just listen to God as He speaks right into your heart.

Perhaps right now you are feeling forsakenness or being separated from God. Amazingly God Himself knows what this is like. It is called the Immanuel Paradox. Immanuel or God with us experiences separation from God on the cross for bearing our sinfulness. God is forsaken by God in other words so how can this be? It really means that God is with us even in times of feeling utter forsakenness and separation from Him. He is with us in our forsakenness because He knows the reality of it. Even in our darkest hours, God is with us and perhaps especially so, having experienced a depth of separation on the cross we can never experience. No matter what depth of darkness we experience, Immanuel is with us.

God makes such a wonderful promise to us in Deuteronomy 1: 29-31. He describes Himself as a father who carries His children in His arms and fights for us. When does a father carry his child in his arms? When perhaps the child is very young and learning to walk. When perhaps the child is unwell or lost or confused. When the child is hurt and needs protection and healing comfort. Whenever the child may be fearful or troubled the father carries them in his arms of love. Why does Almighty God use such an illustration to us? He wants us to know and experience safety and security in His loving arms. He wants us to know love and the protection of being close to His heart. He wants us to be confident that we will reach our destination carried by Him. A father may also carry his child one more time, when the child dies. God will carry us across death into His heavenly homeland and into eternal life when we die. We will not see death but God in all His glory. This is most beautiful and a real word of comfort from our wonderful Father, who carries us daily in His loving arms.

Father God is our destination according to Jesus in John 14: 1-7. When we come home, we come home to the Father. Jesus is the journey to the Father where our true home lies because the Father loves us passionately, energetically, thoughtfully and strongly. He wants us to learn to love Him in the same way and with the same intensity that He loves us. Luke 16: 13. To be at home with Father is to enter fully into the love relationship He wants us to enjoy with Him forever. This is why Jesus prays for us in John 17: 1-3, saying to know God and experience Him is eternal life. God is so amazing and full that it takes all eternity to completely know Him. Eternal life is coming home to the Father and Jesus so we can know, enjoy and delight in them forever. This is what it means to have an eternal relationship with our Creator. We will forever delight in Him and the things He delights in forever.

What is the heart of the gospel message and how can we communicate this to a broken world? Is the Church not a redeeming and reconciling community because of the good news revelation we have received from God? The Son of God became the Son of Man in order that sons of men might become sons of God. Every day we have a fresh and new beginning with God and an opportunity to encounter Him like never before. The amazing truth is that saved sons and daughters are now God's ambassadors called to represent our God here on earth. We are called to represent Him and given His authority to do so well. God is taking a big step in asking us to be His ambassadors but He is full of faith for us and promises to anoint us to fulfil the mission and call. He is setting us an example of how to live by faith. He gives us the signet ring of sonship, the robe of righteousness and the sandals of authority to walk where He walks. Luke 15. What an honour, what a privilege and what a wonderful gracious heavenly Father we have. He wants us to represent Him on earth in the power of the Holy Spirit, sent from heaven to equip us to serve Him excellently. Why don't you bow your head in praise and worship before Father right now and thank Him for calling you to be His ambassador and ask Him to anoint you afresh to fulfil the call. 2 Corinthians 5.

In Psalm 85: 6-13 we have a prophetic song written by the sons of Korah all about revival. It is a fresh start with God as He gives us a new taste of His joy and gladness. It is God pouring out even more of His love on us as He restores us back to Himself. Revival is God pouring out His presence and power on us as His glory hovers over us. Blessing after blessing rains down from above as God drenches the land with a bountiful harvest of righteousness and souls. I had a dream recently where God spoke to me saying I was a driver for revival. I know I will see and taste it before God calls me home and nothing excites me more. Please meditate on this wonderful Psalm 85 because I believe there are hidden keys in it for revival, it is a blueprint for revival psalm and word from God for the Church to cling to and pursue.

Arrogant, aggressive, militant paganism seems to be the fertile seed bed for revival because the people of God are desperate for God to move supernaturally to turn things around in Church and nation. This is the cry of the prophet in 2 Chronicles 7: 14 and the heart of God responds with the great promise for revival for both the people and the land. It is the cry of David as he pens Psalm 24 to God's living gateways and ageless doors of destiny among His chosen people both Jews and Gentiles. He is about to come through armed and ready for battle, the Mighty One invincible in every way. We need to waken up, rejoice and fling wide for the King of Glory to enter and take the nations back to Himself. The world belongs to God, everyone and everything belongs to Him and He has set a time in history when He will return to take it all back again.

Beloved friends, what should be our proper response to God's marvellous mercies? Romans 12: 1-21. TPT. Surrender to God to be His sacred, living sacrifices. Live in holiness, experiencing all that delights His heart. For this becomes your genuine expression of worship. Stop imitating the ideals and opinions of the culture around you, but be inwardly transformed by the Holy Spirit through a total reformation of how you think. This will empower you to discern God's will as you live a beautiful life, satisfying and perfect in His eyes. When we are totally surrendered to God then everything we think is totally transformed. This leads to reformation, revival and transformation because we are what we think. Paul goes on to warn us about pride the sin of the devil. Isaiah 14 and Ezekiel 28. We must assess our self- worth and value before God by faith in what He tells us about who we are in His Word. This in turn gives us an appropriate self-esteem. Each one of us believers by the grace of God has a valuable and unique role to play in the Body of Christ. God's marvellous grace imparts to each one of us varying gifts and ministries that are uniquely ours.

Prophets, teachers, servers, encouragers, givers, leaders and caregivers are the seven categories of Paul's focus for us to consider. The spark that ignites each gift is faith as the Body of Christ becomes devoted to loving and caring for one another. A transformed relationship with God supernaturally produces a transformed relationship with other people, both believers and unbelievers, as God teaches us how to relate to others in a Christlike manner. Romans 12: 9-21. We are to do our best to live at peace with all people and speak blessing over all people rather than a curse. Romans 12: 14.

In chapter 13 Paul goes on to speak about our relationships with God's ordained authorities because he wants us to be people who enjoy the favour and blessing of God in our daily lives. We are to be good citizens having a powerful witness for Christ by doing what is good and right by way of the ordained authorities. We must keep the law of the land we are called to live in unless that law clashes with God's. We must work to pay our taxes and provide for our families so as not to depend on a godless state system. The only debt we should have as believers is to continually love one another for love fulfils all that the law of God requires. We are living in a strategic hour of human history so we need to waken up for our full salvation is nearer now than when we first believed. There is a full salvation ready to be unveiled and unfolded in the last days. 1 Peter 1: 5. We need to fully immerse ourselves into the Lord Jesus, the Anointed One for such a time as this.

Love is the key to unity as we accept and embrace one another with spiritual maturity. We each have the ability to empower others to do what is right and good for them, and to bring them into spiritual maturity. Now may God, the source of great endurance and comfort, grace you with unity among yourselves, which flows from your relationship with Jesus, the Anointed One. Then, with a unanimous rush of passion, you will with one voice glorify God, the Father of our

Lord Jesus Christ. You will bring glory when you accept and welcome one another as partners, just as the Anointed One has fully accepted you and received you as His partner. Romans 15: 1-7.

Romans 15: 13 is one of my favourite verses in the Scriptures because it is full of amazing revelation about the heart of God. He is the God who is the source of our hope. I meet many people in the city centre devoid of hope and when I do, I try to fill them with hope by telling them the truth about God and His love for them. God designed us to be full of hope through relationship with Him so without Him it is little wonder we have no hope. He wants to fill us completely with joy and peace as we learn to trust in Him because He is our good, good Father. We will overflow with abundant rivers of hope to others as a result of our hope in God. Confident hope comes through the witness of the Holy Spirit in us and through us to others without hope. This is a very powerful thing as God anoints us as His witnesses. Acts 1: 8. Will you go out today and be a source of hope to others through your own hope in God? You have far too much to keep it all to yourself so you must overflow through the power of the Holy Spirit. True hope is supernatural coming from the God who formed and made us for Himself. We have the wonderful hope of eternal life through Jesus Christ our Lord for this life and the next and this world desperately needs to hear this message. Be a source of hope wherever God asks you to travel in this world and hold it out to others as you cross their paths daily.

I share the joy of working alongside people who once had no hope but now have hope and their stories with the God of hope are inspirational and wonderful. I have witnessed first- hand how God uses their stories of hope to continually inspire the homeless and marginalised in Glasgow and beyond. Many of them used to live on the streets trapped in the bondage of hopelessness and addiction until God broke through for them with real hope. Now they are taking their personal messages of hope out to others and it is awesome to see how God uses them as overflowers of confident hope. To each and every one of them I say thank you for being such an amazing inspirational source of hope for others. Great will be your rewards in heaven and upon earth faithful children of God.

You are reading this today and thinking how you can be a source of hope to others around you. Just be yourself in Christ and God will use you as you are. Just reach out lovingly and Holy Spirit will open the hearts of others up to you as they sense God's love in you. Just be there to listen and offer help whenever opportunity arises and God will do the rest. It is because you trust in Him that confident hope flows through you and will overflow out to them. This is God's promise to you so why don't you memorise this verse and learn to use it in prayer for yourself and others as it inspires your faith. Romans 15: 13.

— 15 —

H'S STORY

Psalm 119: 71 KJV. It was good for me that I have been afflicted, that I might learn thy statutes.

Whenever I am asked to share testimony, I always cast my mind back to my childhood and try to think what happened in my life that made it take the course it did. Was it the separation of my parents at a young age? Was it lack of discipline from my parents? Was it the lack of money in my family? I could say many different things but ultimately it was the bad judgements and decision making I made even though as a child I had done many childish things but for the most part I had a very blessed and protected upbringing.

The bad decisions and judgements I mentioned were the type that brought instant gratification with total disregard for consequences and made me feel good. I was not at all interested in anybody who would try to have a positive impact on my life, indeed I treated them with total contempt. As I sit here now with a clear head and Jesus in my heart, I can clearly identify thinking and behaving as I used to was the start of a massive spiral downwards in my life. If anybody tried to explain then that my thinking was sinful and selfish, I would have laughed in their face or even lashed out at them physically.

By now you are probably building an image of how my life was going and this was before I had even left school, where I achieved enough to be accepted into college for further study. To me these were things that did not give me that instant buzz so in my immaturity I rubbished them and followed a path of self -destruction by lying, stealing and drug using as I left school to find a well -paid job. This was like pouring fuel on an already blazing fire and my drug usage and experimentation increased more and more.

Almost 15 years of addiction would follow with short sporadic periods of being clean through periods of being in and out of prison. I tried so many things to break the cycle of addiction with limited success. I tried going cold turkey and secular rehabs along with prescribed medications like the methadone programme when I was locked up but nothing seemed to work longer term for me. Addiction had become the only friend who comforted me in times of real desperation and trouble. My narrow mind was always centred on the temporal not the eternal. I should have died many times through overdoses and scuffles with other drug users. I vaguely remember being in the back of an ambulance with two paramedics standing over me and my mother as my heart had stopped beating and I can now thank God for keeping me alive for His purposes.

Then one night I had a meeting in the street where I was begging, with two people from a local church. They took me to their outreach café for a hot drink and some food to eat and treated me like a real human being. I was shown kindness and love I did not deserve that night. I wrote this off as a chance but over the next few months I would bump into these same people over and over again, was befriended by them and invited into their church. In the presence of these people a seed was being planted of hope and a future for me without drugs. Eventually I was led to the Lord with many tears not fully understanding what I was doing or what would change in my life. I was offered the chance to go to a Christian rehab and woke up the next morning in a strange surrounding where I walked downstairs to find twenty men singing happy birthday to me! If it wasn't for my withdrawal symptoms being so bad, I would have left but thankfully I chose to stay.

This turned out to be the single best decision I ever made in my life. Over the next 18 months I learned what It meant to ask Christ to be Lord of my life. I had begun a journey I am still on today as seeds planted in the church take root and reform my attitudes and values towards God, myself and others. I learned that Jesus had to come first not me and that was a bitter pill to swallow at first. Change does not come easy but the willingness to change was there and this gave God permission to work in my life. Now my eyes are fixed on the eternal and not just the temporal. I have been to some amazing places all over the world and made many new friends in the process, something I could never have imagined at the beginning of my journey of faith. I can only be amazed and stand in awe of God with gratitude for that night of encounter on the city streets and now I am a married man with a beautiful wife and family living on a beautiful estate. Only God could do something like that.

I pray that as you read this you will realise that there is, no place God's hands of salvation cannot reach and no heart He cannot touch and change as you are loved by Him unconditionally. Shalom and blessings to you all from H a man changed and blessed by the Living God.

16

JEREMIAH

J eremiah was a priest and a prophet. He lived under the rule of king Josiah of Judah and enjoyed a season of political and religious revival from 627 to 609 BC. Jeremiah has a lot to teach us about political and religious revival, two things desperately needed in the United Kingdom today. His calling by God is recorded in Jeremiah 1: 4-19. He received a very personal word of calling verse 4. It was a word revealing to him God's plans and purposes for his life from beginning to end. However, God reveals things to him in verse 5 applicable to all of us. All of God's children are known and approved as His chosen instruments. We are separated and set apart as consecrated for God's works and finally we are appointed and anointed for all God plans for us to do. These are wonderful truths encouraging us to always remain in alignment to God's plans for our lives because when we do, we cannot fail. Psalm 62: 2 and 6 TPT. In these final days before Christ's return, we are called to live as those separated, set apart, consecrated, appointed and anointed. Like Jeremiah, you may feel overwhelmed by the tasks at hand but God is with you and you shall not fail.

God is putting His Words in your mouth and giving you His authority to root out, pull down, destroy, overthrow, build and plant. Jeremiah 1: 6-10. Declare and speak out the words God has given you over your life and situation and things will change according to the authority behind God's Word and yours as they become one and the same. God also gifted the young Jeremiah to see in the Spirit as well as prophesy, he was a prophet and Seer just like king David. We need Seers and Prophets again today to deliver the words of God to our Church and nation. Will you be one of them? God watches over His Word, alertly and actively, to perform it. God loves to perform on the stage of His creation and demonstrate His glory, majesty and power. God will fulfil every single promise ever made to nations and individuals everywhere through faith. Stand on the promises God has given to you in the Bible, confidently, expectantly and prayerfully and watch God perform them.

Look at the personal nature of the promise God gives to Jeremiah in 1: 18-19. He is to expect opposition but also victory. He is promised divine strength and ultimate deliverance because God is with him and will never leave or forsake him. Hebrews 13: 5. God asks a question in 2: 11. Has a nation ever changed its gods, even though they are not gods? Here in the United Kingdom the people have changed their Glory God for that which does not profit. As society breaks down and moves further and further away from God's truth, we are forsaking the God of the Word our Fountain of Living Waters. We are choosing broken cisterns unable to satisfy. We have forsaken the Lord our God and are indifferent to Him and without fear or respect for Him anymore as a nation. Jeremiah 2: 19. God called the United Kingdom to be a nation serving Him and His purposes but we have long departed from the calling and are destined for judgement unless we repent and revival sweeps through the nation again. But God gives us a revival promise in Jeremiah 3: 15-18 and 4: 1-2. Will you pray this with me for our nation? God is looking to answer the prayers of just one uncompromisingly righteous person. Jeremiah 5: 1. Will you be that person?

God continually speaks to His people through Jeremiah and in 9: 23-24, he receives revelation about the character of God and the call to walk with God personally. To understand and know God personally and practically is the only way to experience meaning in this life. Solomon writes the whole of the book of Ecclesiastes to reveal this to us and he was the wisest man who has ever lived on the face of the earth apart from Jesus. We must invest our lives in the eternal not the temporal and be faithful stewards of all the resources given us by God. Look at Jeremiah 10: 10-16 and 17: 5-10. What is God saying to you through these Scriptures? Look at Jeremiah 17: 12-14 and ask yourself has God saved and healed you?

When we find and eat God's Words and they become our joy and the rejoicing of our hearts we then know we are called by His Name and have the authority to act and speak as ambassadors for Jesus. Jeremiah 15: 16. We are invited to stand in the council of the Lord in Jeremiah 23: 18 and hear His word. We must do this daily to be effective ambassadors for Jesus. Jeremiah 29: 11-14 is a promise given to us when we discipline our lives to stand in His council and hear and obey His words. He deserves nothing less. He alone releases us from the captivity of sin, bondage and addiction to bring us back to Himself for all addiction is sin and idolatry where we place self before God and His will for our lives. Jeremiah 33: 3.

In Jeremiah 18 God tells the prophet to go down to the house of the potter and watch him working his wheel. The vessel was initially spoiled in the potter's hands but then reworked and revived. The United Kingdom can be reworked and revived in God's mighty hands. Here is a promise to our nation in 18: 7-10. There is still time for God to speak to the nation and turn us back to Himself. Jeremiah 23: 29. His Word is like fire that consumes all that cannot endure the test and like a hammer breaking the rocks of resistance to rubble. Let us take the promises of God and cry out to Him for ourselves, our families, our Church and nation that God would rework, reawaken and revive us again to His great salvation plans and purposes.

I want us to look at some chapters in the Bible that are full of questions and another book that seems to be written to ask the deep questions we all ask. In Isaiah 40 there are 22 questions in just 31 verses. The first question arises in verse 6. What should I shout? He is told to shout Good News from the mountain tops so all could hear. He is shouting to the people to get ready and be prepared for a visitation of God and His presence among them. "Your God is coming". He is coming in power. He will rule with a powerful arm. Yet for all His mighty power God promises to gently lead the mother sheep with their young as a gentle Shepherd. The whole earth is compared to a grain of sand held in God's hand a hand so big it spans the entire universe as it measures of the heavens with His fingers. God is saying He has no equal and no comparison and He is asking so many questions in this chapter to reveal to us that compared to Him, we are utterly nothing, mere emptiness and froth. He is saying don't get too big for your boots, remember who you are and who I AM and relate to me with reverence and fear.

Although God is so majestic and glorious, He still sees our troubles and does not ignore our rights. He loves His chosen people, Jew and Gentile and promises to anoint us with supernatural power to serve Him and carry out His assignments. Isaiah 40 must be one of the greatest chapters in the Bible for revealing the nature, character and glory of God. Now look at Job 38 to 41: 6. God is asking His servant Job 70 questions without even giving him time to answer one of them. Job had seriously aggravated God and this was His way of bringing him to repentance. It is as if God wants to overwhelm Job with questions, He knows he cannot answer. God is about to overwhelm Job with His presence, power and glory as he stands naked and bruised before Him. God brings His suffering child to repentance and a new depth of trust in Him before blessing his life twice as much as before his suffering began. He asks Job to pray for his three friends who had just heaped insults on him and blasted him with condemnatory comfort and then as Job obeys, the floodgates of heaven are once again opened all over his life. I think you will agree with me when I say it is good and very important for us to listen to God when He asks us questions.

In Luke 12, Jesus asks a total of twelve questions and Peter one. Jesus is asking us to consider the spiritual significance of the times we are living in. He wants us to be ready and prepared for His return and not asleep or living carelessly. Jesus is constantly asking questions and making statements all through Luke 12. Again, He is using the questions to reveal truth. He deals with anxiety and worry, the Kingdom realm, worldly wealth and stewardship and our witness and how we should defend ourselves. He deals with false teaching, religiosity, exposure and our need to continually trust in God. Right in the middle of the chapter He speaks about birds and wild flowers using them as an example for us to follow as we learn to depend on God for everything we need in life. The point He is making is that birds and wild flowers are important to God but not as important as His beloved children, so we can depend on His provision completely.

In Ecclesiastes we have a book written by the wisest man on earth at the time, King Solomon. Why would Solomon write a book from the perspective of unbelief when he clearly had faith in God? We know from the books of Proverbs, Song of Songs and 1 Kings 3: 1-28 that Solomon was a man of God, who had a personal encounter with God through a dream. Is Ecclesiastes included in the Bible to ask questions which the rest of the Bible answers? The book begins where people are and the rest of the Bible takes us to where God wants us to be. In Ecclesiastes the Bible brings to the surface the questions that lie deep in every human heart. The answer to all of the questions posed in Ecclesiastes are found in Christ the Messiah.

In John 6 Jesus is revealing to us that He is the Living God and the Bread of Life come down to earth from heaven. In John 6: 28 a question is posed. So, what should we do if we want to do God's work? God's work is to believe rather than strive for perfection which we can never attain. Jesus is here saying that faith and belief in Him is all God requires from us in order to have eternal life. He is saying that the Father's passion is to share eternal life with us through our believing in His Son and His sacrifice for us on the cross. This is so simple and profound and yet so easy to miss. Many people saw Jesus and even His miracles and yet they did not choose to believe in Him. Jesus came down from heaven as a loaf of bread and a cup of wine for us to enjoy as He is the Living God and the Bread of Life, so that all God requires of us is satisfied by the sacrifice of Jesus on the cross. The Christ in us is enough to satisfy God. Belief in Him is enough, no striving is needed, just trust and belief. The work which pleases God more than any other is the work of belief in His Son's sacrifice for us. The Father is pleased and happy with you today because you believe. Our primary purpose is to believe and allow our belief to shape and conform us into Christlike people. God's primary assignment for us humans is that we believe.

As we open the door of our hearts and believe by inviting Christ in, we are promised a feast with Him. Revelation 3: 20. Jesus did a lot of feasting during His life on earth, it was something He loved to do as He showed love and warmth to other people. He did this to be known and to know or to develop relationships with other people. In Leviticus 23 we see God's seven feasts given to the Hebrew people as special occasions to experience relationship with God. I believe these seven feasts are God's seven priorities because they are revelations of the full redemptive purposes of God.

The Feast of Passover in Leviticus 23: 5 celebrates the blood of the lamb and the salvation made possible by God for His people as the angel of judgement passed over Egypt. It looks ahead to the blood of the Lamb of God paying the price for the salvation of all men having faith in Him. God's first priority is blood because without sinless, blameless blood His justice cannot be satisfied. Christ's sinless blood purchased, pardoned and paid for us on the cross as we believe in Him. It all begins here in Leviticus through the blood sacrifice.

The Feast of Unleavened Bread celebrates relationship with God and other believers made possible by the blood. It celebrates new relationships vertically and horizontally as in the shape of a cross. Leviticus 23: 6-8. We can celebrate that our sins are washed away by the spotless blood and remembered no more.

The Feast of First fruits, celebrates the resurrection life now made possible for us through Christ's resurrection. He is the first fruit of all of a new creation of family belonging to God who will follow Him and enjoy eternal life with Him. He is the last Adam renewing all of the blessings of God for people lost under the sin of the first Adam. Leviticus 23: 9-14.

The Feast of Harvest or Pentecost celebrates the bringing in of the harvest as the Holy Spirit is poured out on the people of God and we are empowered to share the Gospel in all the nations. Leviticus 23: 15-22.

The Feast of Trumpets celebrates the going and telling or the witness of the people of God to the nations as we trumpet sound the good news far and wide all across the nations. Leviticus 23: 23-25. We are His witnesses. Acts 1: 8.

The Feast of Atonement celebrates the fact that Christ's sacrifice for us is eternal and evermore sufficient to wash away sin and bring us into the holy presence of God. The Way is forever opened up for us to come through Christ's atoning blood which He took into heaven and sprinkled in the sanctuary of God on our behalf. It is a once and for all time and eternity sacrifice continuously available and speaking for us. Book of Hebrews and especially 10.

Feast of Shelters Leviticus 23: 33-44 celebrates the promise of Christ's return and reminds us to be ready and prepared because this world is not our true resting place. God is calling us to feast on Him and with Him. In His wisdom, God has summarised His whole redemption plan in the annual feasts given to His chosen people and celebrated before the world for centuries. God is speaking to us through these feasts, they are His witness and a prophetic declaration of His intent. As God invites you to open your heart to Jesus and invite Him in through the open door, He is promising to feast with you because He is passionately in love with you. Why don't you stop what you're doing right now and celebrate the goodness of God and invite Him in to enjoy a feast with you. Seven is God's perfect number in Scripture and the seven feasts are established to bring us into a perfect relationship with God through faith in the atoning blood sacrifice of Jesus. As He fills us with resurrection hope and power through the coming of the Holy Spirit, we will share in the harvest of souls still to be reaped, and along with them we will be ready and prepared for the return of Christ, and the establishing of the Kingdom of God, where we will reign with Him forever.

I hear the Spirit saying somebody is reading this right now and you don't feel ready for Christ's coming, it actually fills you with fear and anxiety when you think about it. If this is you then I ask you to join with me in this prayer to the Father as He comes by His Spirit to minister grace, love and mercy to us right now...

Heavenly Father I come before you to be washed anew and afresh in the sinless blood of Christ Your Son given to me. Today I repent and turn back towards You and away from all sin and sinful relationships with people and things. I now invite the Holy Spirit into my heart to fill me and empower my witness anew for Christ. I ask for gifts of the Spirit to help me to witness powerfully for You. I give myself over to You completely and confess You as my Lord and I now put You into the driving seat of my life. I believe in You and want to serve you for the rest of my life. Speak to me clearly as I read and think about Your Words in the holy Bible and may they become Your love letter to me. Wrap me into Christ's death, resurrection and seating with You in the heavenly realms and give me a new hunger and thirst to know You more and love other people. I ask these things in the Name of Jesus the Christ, Amen.

17

REVELATIONS FROM
THE ETERNAL GOD

J ohn the Apostle was invited to ascend into the heavenly realm to
receive revelations from God. Revelation 4: 1-11. Instantly he was
there and in just eleven verses John speaks about God's throne fourteen
times. God's throne is the governmental centre of the universe. He is
seated on His throne glowing a blood red colour known as Carnelian
or Sard. God is sparkling, glowing and has an emerald rainbow halo
around Him. This represents the mercy and covenant loves of God
and reminds us that everything He does is surrounded with grace and
mercy. Why would God choose to glow a blood red colour if not to
signify the precious shed blood of His Son on the cross?

God's throne is encircled, by twenty- four others, each with a
believer having white garments and golden crowns. They represent
all believers clothed in Christ's righteousness and crowned with glory.
Four mysterious living creatures worship God without ceasing night
and day, one with a human face, one resembles a lion, another an ox
and another an eagle in flight. These creatures have six wings and are
covered in eyes, even under their wings. What a most wonderful scene
John is shown here at the very centre of the universe. The question is,

did we exist in the heavenly realm in some form before being created by God? David seems to hint that we did in Psalm 23 verse 6 in the Passion Translation when he declares he will return to God to be forever with him following this life. The children of God were created by plan in heaven to exist on the earth before returning to be with our God forever.

Solomon tells us that God planted His heavenly seed within us in Ecclesiastes 3: 11. Eternity has been planted in our hearts and minds to stamp us with eternal destiny. We were hot-wired to know and be known by our Creator God in other words. The human soul hungers and thirsts for the love of our Creator. We were never designed to be separated from Him. God planted the divine seed of His purpose in us and nothing but He can satisfy this divine longing and homecoming. This is both wonderful and mysterious. David is saying he is returning to God's glorious presence from which he came. He is saying every child of God existed in some form in the heart and mind of God before being birthed into both physical and eternal reality. When we are born again or born from above, we are aligning our earthly reality to our heavenly and eternal reality. This is one of the most wonderful things which God has done from beginning to end but out with our minds to comprehend says Solomon. Ecclesiastes 3: 11b.

Jude declares that God keeps us from falling away and brings us into His glorious presence with great joy and without a single fault. Jude 24, 25. Our God, seated on His governmental throne of the universe, glowing in blood red Carnelian, planned and birthed each one of us into an earthly and heavenly destiny. No wonder David declares, so why should we fear the future? What is God saying to us here from the heart declarations of these two anointed men of God? We may be experiencing the heights of Psalm 23 or the depths of Ecclesiastes but our eternal destiny is secure and safe nonetheless. God has birthed us through blood red into our eternal destiny with a glory, majesty, power and authority beyond all time and the age of man. We are an eternal part of His love story and the best is yet to come. Time does not define the children of God, for we are eternal beings with eternal destiny. Our future is safe and secure in the hands and plans of our God. And now all glory to God! We confidently and joyfully look forwards to sharing God's glory. Romans 5: 1-2.

In Exodus 3: 1-15 the Holy Spirit records Moses' encounter with God and in the process, we are all given a revelation of God. The most sacred name for God in Hebrew is YHVH, Yud, Heh, Vav, Heh. God is the I AM. In Psalm 103: 1-5, David says, let all that I am praise the Lord the I AM. God is our source of life and the reason for our existence because there is a flow to existence and the source of the flow is I AM. He existed before anything and everything He created and when we say our name for example, I am Stephen, I am confessing His Name before my own for I came from Him and I will return to Him. Psalm 23: 6. Every time we say I am we are confessing His great Name and declaring He is the source of all life and existence. This is true for all mankind whether we acknowledge Him as I AM or not. This is why Jesus is the Judge of all men and when we die, we have an immediate appointment with Him. He is the source of our life and we are all accountable to Him. 2 Corinthians 5: 10 and Hebrews 9: 27. The natural order of life as created by God is to put Him first not ourselves, for we flow from His existence and will return to Him. And afterwards, when my life is through, I will return to Him to be with Him forever. Psalm 23: 6 TPT.

When we meditate on Psalm 103: 1-5 we notice that all of the promises given are constant and continuous. He forgives all our sins and heals all our diseases. He redeems us from death and crowns us with love and tender mercies. He fills our lives with good things our youth is renewed like the eagle's. God is continuously renewing our spirits, souls and bodies, so that we can continue to praise Him with all our hearts. Here comes the question. How could I ever forget the good things He does for me? David makes a list of all the good things God does for us all. The word all is most important for God forgives all our sins and heals all our diseases. Before we can be crowned, we must be redeemed. A crown awaits all who are redeemed. He forgives, He heals, He redeems, He crowns, He fills, He renews, He gives righteousness and justice verse 6. God is continuously doing all of these wonderful things for us because He is compassionate and merciful, slow to get angry and filled with unfailing love, verse 8. He is now revealing His character to us just as He revealed it to Moses. He wants to fill our lives with good things so we have no desire or room to sin for the wages of sin is death but the gift of God is eternal life through Jesus Christ our Lord. The reason we exist is to praise the Lord with all our hearts for all the good things He has done for us. His redemption promises are constant and continuous, past, present and future as we determine to continuously walk with Him in the faith of them. Now all glory to God, who is able to keep us from falling away and who will bring us into His glorious presence with great joy and without a single fault. Jude 24. The life flowing from God the I AM into us is continuous and constant like a river of living water constantly living and moving. He is renewing our lives at all levels so why should we fear the future? He is the source of all life and all things good which means our lives are safe and secure in His eternal hands. Even if you have been treated unfairly the Lord promises to give you righteousness and justice at His chosen time. He has separated your sins from you as far as east is from west, which is an eternal distance, for there is no pole at east or west, as there is at north and south. What a wonderfully good and kind Father we have as He lavishes everything heaven contains upon us all because we are united to and wrapped into His Son, Jesus Christ. Ephesians 1: 3. Why don't you spend some time right now worshiping God and praising Him for all He is doing for you and remember it is past, present and future for He has called you into eternal life. All glory, majesty, power and authority are His before all time, and in the present, and beyond all time! Amen. Jude 25.

When God planted eternal awareness in us, He did so to tell us we are eternal beings with an eternal calling and destiny. A seed is planted to grow, flourish, leaf and fruit in the soil and rain of God's promises. Isaiah 55. He is our ever green, fruitful tree and we are His seeds, spread all over the earth to leaf and fruit and so others can taste and see that the Lord is good. Hosea 14: 8-9. There is an ache for God which throbs at the core of our being and nothing but He can satisfy this emptiness. A vacuum exists in our souls without God. Jeremiah the prophet tells us that we were designed to hunger and thirst for God our

Creator. Jeremiah 17: 5-14. Because God has planted into our hearts, we are both time and eternity aware and driven to thirst for God. We are created to enjoy an intimate love relationship with our Creator and Redeemer. This is what He wants for us and what we want from Him. A future without God is described as hopeless, like a shrub growing in a barren, salty, wilderness or a desert land, where we are constantly thirsty but never satisfied, lost and wandering aimlessly. Does this describe your life right now? Many choose to reject God and live in this barren wilderness of spirit and soul, even as they enjoy material things for a short season but there is so much more when we look upwards to God. To reject God brings a curse and no prospect of an eternal hope so which would you rather be a stunted shrub or an evergreen fruitful tree? Jeremiah describes God as a fountain of living water and as we come to drink from Him the drink becomes a river of living water equipping us for this life and the next.

A righteous life is always a fruitful life because the seeds of righteous living always produce fruits in every season of life. Our tree roots need to grow deeper and deeper into the water of the Spirit and His Word because deeply rooted trees survive and thrive in the storms of life raging all around us. Now is the time to write down a letter to God asking Him to outdo your greatest request, most unbelievable dream and wildest imagination. To invite God to achieve infinitely more in excess of them all as His miraculous power energizes you. Ephesians 3: 14-21 TPT.

Now may the God of peace make you holy in every way, and may your whole spirit and soul and body be kept blameless until our Lord Jesus comes again. God will make this happen, for He who calls you is faithful. 1 Thessalonians 5: 23-24. God makes things happen. He is the God of peace who is faithful. Jesus Christ is our pattern for holiness and happiness. Many imagine holiness as complete separation but it is quite the opposite, complete involvement in human affairs without compromise. What do you need God to make happen in your life? As we constantly use our faith, He will respond by making things happen. We have a question on the streets frequently asked of one another, what's happening? We want to know what God is doing in each of our lives as we serve Him together. God is both the cause and the effect, the One making things happen.

Deuteronomy 10: 12-22 asks the question, what does the Lord require of you? He requires that you fear the Lord your God and live in a way that pleases Him, and love Him and serve Him with all your heart and soul. The Hebrew word used here for fear means worship, awe, reverence and submission. It is the same word used in Job 28: 28 where Job declares something really special in response to two questions asked twice in Job 28. The questions are but do people know where to find wisdom? Where can they find understanding? If God says it once, it is to be believed. If He says it twice, it demands our utmost attention. Job 28: 12 and 20. We are told that wisdom and understanding are not found among the living, verse 13. That God alone understands the way to them, verse 23. God has evaluated wisdom, set it in place and examined it thoroughly, verse 27. As a result of His thorough evaluation of wisdom, God has a message to all humanity which demands our utmost attention. The fear of the Lord is true wisdom; to forsake evil is real understanding. Job 28: 28. If wisdom is not found among the living it must have a supernatural origin in God. In Proverbs 1: 1-7, Solomon writes about words of wisdom and kingdom revelations, telling us to live by them as they empower us with spiritual understanding. True knowledge is like opening a treasure chest packed with the most valuable treasures in the universe. The treasures help us to understand our design and destiny and give us discernment to acquire brilliant strategies for leadership. They also help us to demonstrate wisdom in all our relationships.

The fear of the Lord is true wisdom and when we are living in a relationship with God characterised by worship, awe, reverence and submission, we are living in the fear of the Lord. This Hebrew word for fear is used fourteen times in Proverbs and the number fourteen represents spiritual perfection. The number fourteen is mentioned three times in the genealogy of Jesus, Matthew 1: 1-17 and is also the number for Passover. The first step to wisdom is a cross shaped step as we submit to God's way of salvation through the cross and receive Jesus Christ as Saviour and Lord to wash away our sins and make us right with God through faith in Him. This is God's wise way and not mans, it is the supernatural way of the cross and it is the wisdom of God. Unless we are willing to submit our wills to God's and come His Way of the cross, we cannot ever learn true wisdom. As we come into a living relationship with God, through the cross, we find ourselves in awe of His grace, mercy and love and fall down before Him in reverent worship. As a consequence of relating to God the Holy One, we find ourselves forsaking evil with real understanding because evil is the very opposite of everything God is and represents.

John the Apostle speaks about this eloquently in his first epistle because he understood that to fear the Lord means lifestyle challenges and changes. How then does a man gain the essence of wisdom? We cross the threshold of true knowledge when we live in obedient devotion to God. Proverbs 1: 7 TPT. In 1 Corinthians 2: 1-16, Paul the Apostle declares that God's wisdom is the mystery of the cross. If the rulers of this world had understood this, they would not have crucified Jesus. God deliberately hid it from them in His wisdom so that His plan could be demonstrated for our ultimate glory. We are not to trust in human wisdom but in the power of God and the cross is the power of God for the salvation of all who believe and have faith. God has made the wisdom of this world look foolish. We cannot know God through worldly wisdom because of the Way of the cross. Christ is the wisdom of God and the power of God. 1 Corinthians 1: 18-31. Christ is wisdom itself for our benefit. As a result, no one can boast in the presence of God. Christ made us right with God, He made us pure and holy and He freed us from sin. If we want to boast we must only boast about the Lord and what He has done and continues to do for us. How I thank God that we believers can understand these things because we have the mind of Christ. As spiritual people we can understand what the Spirit means as He imparts God's truth to us daily. To be Spirit filled is to have access to all the wisdom of God in Christ as we are wrapped into Him permanently. The Spirit searches out everything and shows us God's deep secrets.

Romans 8 is a remarkable chapter where Paul asks seven key questions in just five verses, 31 to 35 NLT. He is determined to show us that every child of God is a child destined for eternal glory. The questions are in order as below:

What should we say about such wonderful things as these? If God is for us, who can ever be against us? Since He did not spare even His own Son but gave Him up for us all, won't He also give us everything else? Who dares accuse us whom God has chosen for His own? Who then will condemn us? Can anything ever separate us from Christ's love? Does it mean He no longer loves us if we have trouble or calamity, or are persecuted, or hungry or destitute, or in danger, or threatened with death?

The wonderful things Paul is speaking about that are ours in Christ are also sevenfold. We are heirs of God. We are joint-heirs with Christ. We are known. We are chosen. We are called. We are justified. We are glorified. To be justified means we are acquitted before the Judge of the universe and found not guilty because we have received what Christ has done for us. We are no longer subject to the wrath of God but saved from it by His grace, love and mercy. Wonderful things indeed bestowed upon us by our wonderful heavenly Father. In Ephesians 1:3, Paul describes these things as every spiritual blessing in the heavenly realms being lavished upon us as we are wrapped into Christ. TPT.

As God's sons and daughters, we are qualified to share all His treasures, including the greatest treasure of all, which is God Himself. This is our inheritance and it is most wonderful. By being joined to Christ we inherit all that He is and all that He has. Our destiny is to be co-glorified with Christ, provided we choose to share His feelings of pain through His sufferings. Both the Holy Spirit and Jesus are praying for our victory and triumph while we fight the good fight here on earth. Nothing in God's universe has the power to diminish His passionate love towards us. There is no power in the universe that could ever be found to distance us from God's passionate love. God cannot stop loving us no more than He can stop loving Jesus. He loves every one of His children equally, consistently and passionately. Why don't you take some time out right now to worship such a wonderful God for all He has done to make you His precious and beloved child. It is not because of any righteous thing we have done but because of His mercy. He reveals His kindness and love to us because He is merciful. He washes away our sins and gives us the Holy Spirit because they are the new birth from above.

Take some time to meditate on the whole of Romans 8 by reading it out loud in perhaps two different versions and you will be blessed as Holy Spirit ministers deeply into your soul by presenting you with a rich banquet to feast upon. Our souls were created to be nourished and strengthened by the living truth of God's words, which are just like food and drink for the soul. The mind or soul controlled by the Spirit is life but the mind or soul still being controlled by the flesh or carnal man is death. God is bringing us up to be children responsive to the Holy Spirit, led and controlled by Him. He is patient with us as we learn from our mistakes in this area. If the willingness is there, God will make it happen. 1 Thessalonians 5: 22,23.

Recently I had a most powerful dream. I was back in Inverness embracing a man whom I used to know, who had been saved there just before me in 1971. As we embraced, I looked up at the sky and saw it was ablaze with fire clouds swiftly moving across it and I heard the words from God, the fire is coming, the fire is coming, the fire is coming! I woke up at this point sobbing and my pillow was soaked with tears. In Revelation 8: 1-5 we see seven Archangels preparing to blow their trumpets. For the new decade ahead, I feel God is saying the very coals of fire from the altar in heaven are going to be thrown down to earth as Christians unite together to pray. God's power will release the Word of the Lord, fresh revelatory divine truth, illumination leading to foundational shakings and purification. God's glory fires are going to cover the earth as the kingdoms of men are shaken to their very foundations by God's power. Fire is coming to purify and sanctify God's Church like never before because a great end times harvest is to be reaped from the nations before Christ returns. Revelation 14: 14-20.

Who are you? Why are you here? Where will you go when you die? You will only find the clear answers to these three key life questions in the Holy Bible. Bible = Basic Instructions Before Leaving Earth. You see your Creator God wants you to know why you are here and where you will go after this short life here on earth. You were designed for a life of love, meaning and purpose, a life full of value and significance. In John 4, the woman at the well Photini, had an encounter with Jesus at a well in the middle of the day that would radically change her life and send her in a completely new direction. She was a religious half-Jew or Samaritan woman but like her empty water jar her life had been full of empty broken relationships. She had been looking for love, acceptance and purpose in all the wrong places. Jesus was waiting for her at the well having sent His disciples away for food into the nearby village. Jesus was both hungry and thirsty not just for physical food and water but for the harvest of souls to come and find eternal life in Him. As He engages with her, He reveals Himself to her as the Messiah and she believes but then she goes back into her village where she had a bit of a reputation and brings them all to Christ. Jesus had sown a spiritual seed into her life and it brought forth an immediate harvest. Photini is recorded in Jewish history as going on to become an evangelist leading her own family to Christ and others in Rome where she eventually died for her faith. She had a religion that did nothing for her because it was dry, empty and unable to satisfy her thirst for love and purpose until she met Jesus. When she realised, she was a daughter of the King of Kings and a child of God, everything changed. What about you have you heard the Father's song over you singing, O My precious child how I love you? This is exactly what He wants you to know and experience right now because your destiny depends on knowing and experiencing His love for you. When you can rest in His love for you then all is well and with God everything is possible.

Get ready for the Day of the Lord or the new age to come when the age of man is over and the nations will be ruled by Christ and His Bride the Church. This Day is described in Joel 2. It begins with the appearance of a mighty army leaving nothing behind them but desolation and destruction. This is an angel army lead by the Commander in Chief the Lord Jesus Christ. He is returning as the victorious King in Psalms 2, 110 and 24. Those who have opposed His coming and reign are to face certain judgement so it is essential that people do so now. Turn to Me now, while there is time, for now is the day of salvation says Yahweh in Isaiah 55. In Joel 2: 1-11, we see that

Jesus has returned and the season of grace is over for the Gentiles but may only be beginning for the Jews. Joel 2: 12-17. Zechariah 14: 1-21 tells us that the armies invading Israel will all be destroyed by some mysteries plague sent by God in judgement. This seems to me to be a season of grace specifically for the Jewish nation to be saved, which will only come when the full number of Gentiles or non-Jews are saved. Romans 11: 26-27.

We need to prepare for the fulfilment of Christ's prophecy in Matthew 24: 9-10. We need to be prepared to endure right to the very end in order to be saved. The earth is about to be shaken by climate changes, epidemics and earthquakes on an unprecedented scale because the new age of the Kingdom of God is coming through the birth pains. A global shaking of the nations is about to occur through seismic events of epic proportion as the new age of the Kingdom of God appears. As I am writing this China has just shut down a city with millions of people due to fears surrounding a new Coronavirus. January 2020. For this new decade we are to trust in the Lord and find new strength, new experiences with God and deeper encounters to prepare us for all that is coming. We must learn to soar higher on wings like eagles in the face of the storms to come. An eagle has great vision, it can spot another soaring eagle from 50 miles away. God wants to increase our vision for the harvest ahead. Eagles are fearless and tenacious as they fly boldly into the storms and use the thermals to soar to greater heights. They use the storms to their advantage and so must we. Eagles are high flyers, soaring to heights of 10,000 feet, where no other bird can survive. They rarely eat dead meat preferring to get their own and this speaks to me about fresh revelation from the Lord on a daily basis by coming nearer and nearer to Him. They possess vitality because they retreat to a mountaintop around 30 and go through a period of metamorphosis where they do not eat for 5 months until the complete change has taken place which adds another 20 years onto their lives. We must use fasting and prayer more regularly to overcome the Devil's strategies and do supernatural wonders with God. Try taking one day weekly to fast and pray with God and others so committed. Eagles nurture their young by being gentle and attentive. They teach them to fly gradually by allowing them to learn what their wings are for. Sometimes this involves letting them fall but the adult birds will always be there to catch them before the fall is fatal. We must teach and guide others like the eagles so that they can survive their first flight.

Amazing encounters with God are waiting for us because we are co-seated with Christ in the heavenly realms, so by faith in God's Word we can go there every day. We need to use our faith daily and switch our spiritual imaginations on in the presence of God as we are worshipping Him. Isaiah had to do this in Isaiah 6 when he found himself caught up in a heavenly encounter with God on His throne. John the Apostle had a similar experience in the throne room, Revelation chapters 4 and 5. These chapters describe what heaven is like and God on His throne is right there in the centre of it all. Isaiah receives a heavenly touch and then he is able to hear God's voice through the smoke and shakings. He went on to receive wonderful prophetic words about the Messiah's sufferings 700 years before they occurred. Isaiah 53. He predicted the virgin birth of Jesus and named Him Immanuel in chapters 7-11. He reveals the seven- fold nature of the Holy Spirit in Isaiah 11: 1-2. In chapter 12 he reveals the wonderful nature of the coming good news gospel of grace message to all mankind.

The first thing John sees in heaven when he goes through the open door is a throne. Everything in heaven emanates from the throne and the One sitting on it. God is glowing brilliantly on the throne and surrounded by twenty- four other thrones, possibly representing the twelve tribes of Israel and the twelve apostles of the Lamb. God's throne is very noisy as it releases thunder, lightning, sounds and voices. This is what Isaiah heard from God's throne, His voice. If you want to hear God's voice come into the throne room with thanksgiving, praise and worship then stay there until God speaks. Psalm 100. The throne is suspended by four seraphim, who worship God unceasing, declaring His eternal nature and holiness. Worship cascades out from the living beings, to the elders, to the angels, then to every creature in heaven, the earth, under the earth and in the sea. This describes a tsunami wave of worship beginning in the throne room of heaven and rippling outwards to embrace all of creation. God and the Lamb are centre of worship in heaven and that open door entered by John the Apostle is still wide open and welcoming for all to come in there after him.

In Psalm 48: 14 TPT we see something really wonderful as the Scripture in the Passion Translation describes a journey or movement through time, into death and onto eternity. We go through time, beyond death, into eternity. Through, beyond, into as a journey.

18

IDOLS

Acts 17: 29 asks us the question, since our lineage can be traced back to God, how could we even think that the divine image could be compared to something made of gold, silver, or stone, sculpted by man's artwork and clever imagination? We must resist imagining God to be like us because the God of the Bible stands apart from His creation and is high above us. We must see God as He reveals Himself to us in the Scriptures and in the Person of the Lord Jesus Christ. We must not create a god out of the darkness of our own hearts for this is idolatry. Paul warns us about this in 2 Timothy 3: 1-5. In these final days Paul tells us that people will reject grace and even pretend to have respect for God, but in reality, they will want nothing to do with His power to transform. In other words, they will choose a god of their own, whom they can control, manipulate and limit. We see this happening today in many churches where many ignore or seek to control the ministry of the Holy Spirit, who is God. People today are calling themselves believers yet they continue to create their own imagination of the Living God by deliberately ignoring or twisting Scriptures to limit His power. This is idolatry and it is happening today right in front of our eyes and leaving us with people calling themselves believers but full of unbelief.

God is limitless, measureless, otherness and we must allow Him to reveal Himself as He is and fear and revere Him. Isaiah 55: 8-9. His thoughts and ways are far higher than ours and far beyond anything we can imagine. Job 28: 28. Let real wisdom and true understanding enter our hearts about who God really is and repent from making Him something or someone like we are. When we see God as one of us, we are more likely to expect Him to act as we do and this can lead to disappointment, when He does not. If we do not deal with disappointment but bury the emotions away, it will resurface at a later date and could wreck our walk with God. Our hope in the Sovereign God of the Bible ought to never lead to disappointment because He is Sovereign and is working to a long- range plan of redemption bigger than we are, which is why our prayers go unanswered sometimes or He just plainly says no. Sometimes God surprises us by using godless people and nations to carry out His plans. This is exactly what Habakkuk discovered when he questioned God about His justice.

In much of society today justice has become corrupted and perverted because the courts hand out puny sentences for major offences and people are left feeling devalued and disappointed. Habakkuk complained to God about violence, evil deeds, misery, destruction and then injustice and then God tells him, He is going to raise up a cruel and violent nation to conquer His own people. Surely this was not the answer Habakkuk expected from a God of justice. God had decided to judge nations through the actions of a people motivated by violence and conquest. The prophet wisely decides to get some time alone with God to seek Him and find out more because he is riled, perplexed and confused by God's revelations. Habakkuk 2: 1. Time to retreat into the watch tower and sit silently in the presence until God speaks to clear away our confusion. Perhaps you are facing a situation right now where this is you and you need to take the same action with God. There is a perversion about injustice today in our nation because the wicked far outnumber the righteous and God's laws are paralyzed. What did God say to Habakkuk to ease his concerns? He told him to live by faith not sight and continue trusting in Him no matter what he could see with his physical eyes because there is always more. Habakkuk 2:

4. God's justice may be delayed for many reasons only known to God but it will suddenly, surely and certainly come for God is just. Those who build cities and kingdoms through corruption and injustice will be held to account by God. The whole earth will be filled with an awareness of the glory of the Lord and every kind of injustice will be exposed and revealed. The Lord's vision given to Habakkuk is an end times vision where the prophet sees God coming and moving to judge the nations. He sees God coming like a mighty warrior dressed for battle with the nations. God is coming to rescue His chosen people and save His anointed ones. The message is that salvation, restoration and deliverance will come for God's people in God's time and at just the right moment.

Rejoice in the Lord, be joyful in the God of our salvation for He is Sovereign and He is our strength. Just as Habakkuk, Asaph the Levite had to get into the sanctuary presence of God in order to understand God's justice. Psalm 73: 16-17. It was only as he entered the Lord's presence in worship that he received revelations about the certainty of his future and others rejecting God. He was enabled to soar on wings as an eagle and see from God's perspective. Psalm 73: 17-28. In Ecclesiastes 7: 13, Solomon encourages us to accept the way God does things, for who can straighten what He has made crooked? God is Potter and we are clay. We must learn to trust Him and not depend on our own understanding when we are confused or struggling with knowing His ways. Proverbs 3: 5-6. Our calling from God is to live by faith especially when we have little or no understanding. God is good and just and by His methods He will act justly and deliver His righteous judgements upon all nations and all mankind.

Psalm 96: 13 and Job 37: 23. The Lord is just and righteous and we should fear and reverence Him. These were Elihu's final words to Job before God appeared to speak to Job from the whirlwind. Whatever God does is right and whatever God does is just. In Zephaniah 3: 17 God is telling us that He is living among us and that He is mighty Saviour. He takes delight in us and rejoices over us with gladness. He renews us with His love and sings songs of joy over us. This is just so beautiful. Why don't you ask God to sing a song of joy over you next time you are in His presence and write down the words of His song. It will help you to feel loved to the very core of your being.

God's story and His glory are much bigger than our wellbeing. We must put a higher value on God's glory than our personal wellbeing to avoid disappointment. God's glory is at stake in the universe. This is exactly the attitude Job showed when he declared Job 13: 15, though He slay me, yet will I hope in Him. Surely, this is also what Jesus did when He surrendered His life to the way of the cross and put a higher value on the Father's glory than His personal wellbeing. He was slain, yet He hoped in Him, who raised Him from the dead.

I believe this coming decade we are going to hear God singing a brand, new song, because He is preparing to come to judge the nations with His justice, truth and righteousness. In Psalm 29 we see God speaking in a very different voice from His still, small voice. He is speaking in a voice that is thunderous, powerful and majestic. It splits, shatters and strikes with lightning bolts. It shakes, quakes and twists. It is the voice of glory, strength and holiness. This is the voice Isaiah heard as the mighty seraphs called out God's Name to one another in the Temple and shook it to its very foundations. Isaiah 6: 3-4. God wants to get the attention of the nations to give them one last opportunity to repent before the coming judgements. He will change the tone of His voice to awaken people to repentance as He reveals the righteousness of the Messiah to every nation willing to listen.

The sufferings and resurrection of the Messiah are His victory and saving power and God is about to release a new symphony with shouting, singing, musical instruments, declaring His good news and wonderful miracles among the nations. Everything created by God has the capacity to praise Him, even the sea, hills, trees, crops, trees, rivers and earth. Psalms 96 and 98 declare this truth marvellously. Just imagine the skies singing for joy and the earth joining in the chorus alongside thunderous oceans and ecstatic fields. Listen to the trees in all the forests lifting up their joyful songs of praise to the Lord. This new song will glorify the Lord by declaring His coming to judge the nations, the world, the earth, with His justice and truth and it is one of God's new songs for the next decade. The Bride will not be singing alone, we will be singing alongside God's creation to awaken mankind to God's coming to live among us. The Lord has announced His victory and has revealed His righteousness to every nation. He has remembered His promise to love and be faithful to Israel. The ends of the earth have seen the victory of our God. Psalm 98: 2-3.

Our proper response to God's marvellous mercies is to worship. All worship is service and all service is worship according to the Hebrew word for worship and work, AVODAH. Apostle Paul calls this the age of fulfilment in Romans 11: 5. He means that God is about to fulfil every prophetic word yet to come to pass in the Scriptures both to Jews and non-Jews. Once the almost full number of Gentiles or non-Jews believes in Messiah the Holy Spirit will shift focus to Jews and all Israel will be saved. Israel's salvation will result in a tidal wave of resurrection power sweeping over the nations again opening up the possibility that more Gentiles as well as Jews can be saved. Romans 11: 15. What a glorious moment in history this will be. Isaiah saw it most beautifully when he wrote Isaiah 59:19-60:3.

God wants us to learn to enjoy Him for who He is as we draw near Him in worship and appreciate Him with reverence, fear and awe. The holiness of God is emphasised more than any other of His attributes in Scripture because it is something He is, His very essence. Heaven is a holy dwelling place because God is there and He will dwell here in the newly created earth in the near future with us, His holy people. The fire that is coming is God's holy, cleansing, purifying, anointing, refining fire described so wonderfully by Malachi in chapter 4. It will consume every evil and shake the nations as well as the Church. Holy Spirit is the Spirit of holiness and to be made holy is liberating and joyful. It is what God created us to know, experience and enjoy in Christ as we are grafted deeper and deeper into Him.

In Titus 3: 1-8 we see God doing twelve marvellous things for us. He reveals His kindness and love to us. He saves, He is merciful, He washes away our sins. He gives us new birth and new life. He gives us the Holy Spirit generously then grace, righteousness and eternal life. May we never forget the good things He does for us. Psalm 103: 2. Just take a few moments to think about these twelve things God has done for you and worship Him thankfully in Spirit and truth.

God's forgiving love is most wonderful. It is love, that motivated God to send Christ so we could be forgiven. Romans 5: 8. Psalm 86: 5 reminds us that God is good, ready to forgive and full of unfailing love to all asking for His help. He has sent His help through Jesus Christ His Son, who gave up His earthly life for us to reconcile us back to God. The blood of Christ is sinless, pure and spotless therefore it makes atonement for us or takes our place before God speaking out Christ's righteousness for us. It is by grace that we are all saved when we believe. All that God requires of us is fully satisfied by the death of Jesus on the cross. The Christ in us is enough to satisfy God.

In Genesis 22: 1-19 we see God testing Abraham's faith by asking him to sacrifice his only son Isaac, the child of the promise. It took Abraham three days to walk with his son to Moriah, the chosen place of sacrifice. I am sure he hoped God would change His mind during this long walk to Moriah but no, it did not happen. Isaac carries the wood on his young shoulders just as God's own Son would carry the wooden cross in the future to the place of sacrifice at Golgotha. Isaac had no idea that he was the burnt offering about to be offered up by his desperate father Abraham. But Abraham believed that Isaac would be raised from the dead immediately and would return with him so his faith did not flinch. What a terrible moment when Abraham tied Isaac to the wood pile and raised his knife to slaughter him. I'm sure he did so with tears of despair flowing down his face. Obedience to God can be very costly. Isaac is spared at the last moment and God rewards Abraham and his seed or spiritual children with multiplication, blessing and victory. Abraham had passed the test and now because of his faith every child of God can inherit the same promises God made to him, this is our spiritual inheritance. Galatians 3; 26-29. Did you really get what I just wrote there, this is most wonderful? You can expect God to honour the same promises He gave to Abraham in your life if you have the boldness to stand on them throughout your life.

Christ is the power of God and the wisdom of God. He has chosen and appointed us to go and produce lasting fruit. John 15: 16. This is an open- door promise given to every appointed child of God. These promises throughout the Bible have to be activated by our faith just as Abrahams were.

Ananias had to be obedient to God for Saul of Tarsus to become Apostle Paul. He had to go find Straight Street, enter the house of Judas and pray for Saul a murderer of Christians. God asked Ananias to use obedient faith and when he did, a Saul became a Paul and history was about to be wonderfully written through the life of a former, forgiven murderer. Acts 9: 10-19. What is God calling you to do through the obedience of faith? It can be something big or smaller it matters not, just do it. Don't underestimate the importance of every little step because all of us have an integral part to play in the purposes and plans of God. I remember sitting on a train one ordinary working day and having my faith tested when God spoke to me by giving me a word of knowledge for the man sitting adjacent to me. It was a word about his mother whom God knew was unwell. I struggled to speak to him for some time because he was reading a newspaper right up high in front of his face so I asked God to cause him to drop the paper and look directly at me. He did so shortly afterwards and I shared the words God had given me for him and his mother. He reacted by immediately lifting the paper back up in front of his face and said nothing for what seemed to me an eternity and I could feel my heart beating wildly in my chest. He then dropped the paper again and told me he was on his way to visit his mom who had COPD and existed on a ventilator. God wanted this young man to know He knew all about their situation and wanted to reassure him about His love and care for them both. The words of faith had been delivered and I knew God would do the rest. God had spoken into the situation through my obedience of faith.

As I thought about this, I realised that this was the Spirit of Elijah, a man just as we are but one full of faith releasing God's supernatural power into his nation. God did things through Elijah that no mere mortal could change because of his faith. He used His servant to declare to other men what God was about to do and as Elijah heard and spoke, so it came to pass because of his obedience of faith. God is releasing this Spirit of Elijah once again to everyone willing to move in the obedience of faith. It is not easy, really risky but great blessing will follow when we obey Him. Will you be a messenger of God in the Spirit of Elijah? When God asks us to speak and declare a thing it shall be done for us and light will shine on the road ahead. Job 22: 28. This new decade will be full of divine declarations through the Church of God as we flow like a river of living water, bringing new life and healing to the nations. The Holy Spirit is once again hovering over the darkness and chaos in order to create the perfect plans and purposes of God for the nations. Genesis 1: 1-5. Psalm 96.

19

GLORY

God is calling us to experience His glory, a revelation only promised to His beloved children. Romans 5: 1-2. Salvation is an experience from God to us as we encounter Him saving us past, present and future. This is as true for Israel as it is for us Gentiles. Praise God, for He has not rejected Israel, whom He has destined for salvation. This is the age of fulfilment when all Bible prophecy will be completely fulfilled. This is tremendously exciting because no other age can claim to have the same expectation as ours. We may live to see the purposes of God for Israel and the Church fulfilled if God allows. Paul reveals Israel's rejection of God's grace gospel as being only temporary and in no way permanent, as some have decided, through an ignorance of Scriptures, especially Romans chapters 9 to 11. There is a divinely chosen remnant of Jewish people receiving salvation by grace, the Messianic Jewish community largely based in Israel. Israel's fullness, restoration, full inclusion, full number will greatly enrich the whole world. Her temporary rejection of Messiah has released the reconciling power of God worldwide, so what will happen when Israel is re-instated and reconciled back to God? It will release resurrection power throughout the whole earth resulting in a massive harvest of souls being saved, healed and delivered all over the nations. Romans 11. 15.

What will this world look like after such a releasing of God's resurrection power? We see in Revelation 7: 9-17 and 14: 14-20 the results. I think multitudes in the valley of decision will be saved and swept into the Kingdom of God. Yahweh is more than ready to save Jewish people, when they turn from unbelief to embrace their Messiah by faith. The mystery is that this partial hardening of Israel, as well as her future salvation, is part of God's plan of salvation for the nations. Romans 8: 28. Paul is joyfully revealing this marvellous truth all across Romans chapters 9-11. We must get this full revelation to have a full understanding and be prepared for this final age of fulfilment. We must continue trusting God's kindness, not falling into unbelief, otherwise, we too may be cut off. God stands before us with kindness in one hand and justice in the other. We must stand before Him in holy reverence, with awe and fear as we see Him moving in fulfilment. We may be sailing into ferocious times of persecution where we must stand strong and remain anchored to the truth of God's holy Scriptures. 2 Timothy 3: 1-17. We are running the final leg of the great relay race of faith, entrusted to take the baton of faith over the finishing line into glory. Run the race, fight the good fight of faith and finish well.

One person with God is in the majority. We see this truth throughout the history of Israel beginning with David's victory against Goliath. Isaiah 63: 1-5a is a prophetic word showing us God is preparing to burst through the heavens and come down. The mountains of unbelief and godlessness will quake in His presence. The fire is coming burning up wooden religions and everything lukewarm. His coming will make nations tremble as His enemies learn the reason for His fame. God is about to do awesome deeds beyond our highest expectations as we see the mountains quake. He is going to work for those who wait for Him. He will welcome those who gladly do good, following His Godly ways. A mountain represents a barrier and stronghold and yet Jesus often climbed mountains to enter into the glorious presence of the Lord, just as Moses in Exodus 19. Mountains can also be places of revelation and divine encounter. The mountains in our lives are going to quake in God's presence as He bursts through and comes down. We are now in a season of divine encounter with El Shaddai, God the Enough and the angel armies, the heavenly hosts sent to serve those faithful to Him. God is coming to work for those whose hearts are entwined to His, those waiting on Him. In His coming down, He will lift us up, to do awesome things with Him. God is not going to allow us to be limited by our expectations, He will simply outdo them all. He is about to do infinitely and immeasurably more. Holy fire is coming so get ready to be a fire starter and keeper.

In Isaiah 6 and John 12: 41 we have some revelation. John is saying that Isaiah saw Jesus Christ as Yahweh high and lofty on His throne before Jesus became incarnate man. In Revelation 1: 10-17, John encounters the Son of Man as King and High Priest in heaven, tending the golden lampstands by filling them with oil, a picture of the Holy Spirit. He is seeing the Holy Spirit being poured into every Church age from Ephesus through to Laodicea, our present age. John falls down at the feet of the risen Messiah as he sees Him as He now is and Jesus lays His right hand upon him to bless him with power, authority and blessing. These are the end times blessings coming to the Church. Psalm 16: 11, 118: 15-16, Isaiah 41: 10, Colossians 3: 1. Jesus is laying His right hand upon us to impart power, authority and blessing to fulfil the coming age, to bring in the full number of Gentiles so that all Israel can be saved. The coming decade will see unprecedented numbers flooding into the Kingdom of God, as Holy Spirit and Church move among the nations, to facilitate God, bursting through the heavens and coming down. The nations are being shaken to prepare us for the coming King and His angel armies. To the only God our Saviour, through our Lord Jesus Christ, be endless glory and majesty, great power and authority from before He created time, now, and throughout all the ages of eternity. Amen. Jude 25. TPT.

Maturity for any child of God is reached when we are moved by the impulses of the Holy Spirit. Sensitivity to the Holy Spirit's agenda is essential to learn to partner with God. Two of us were led by the Holy Spirit down to the river Clyde walk-way in the city centre of Glasgow recently. This can be a very dark place where distressed people are drawn to commit suicide. It is essential that God's people go there regularly to pray and help them, We found a man there drinking and all alone, and asked him if he was okay and wanted to talk. He confessed to us that he had come to commit suicide because he saw no point in going on and he wanted to see his mom again, who had passed away three years earlier. He had recently been hit by a car suffering fractures to his pelvis and shoulder and had difficulty walking. We just listened to his story of life since his mom had passed and began giving him reasons to live rather than die. He warmed to us and allowed us to pray for him and send the spirit of suicide back to hell where it belongs. We were able to comfort him and take him away from the Clyde up to the winter shelter in Dixon Street where we linked him into their support services. It was a great outcome and we were so thankful that we had gone there when we did in response to being led by the impulses of the Holy Spirit. God's timing is always right on time.

When we come to Jesus and drink, we become a river of living water to help others in need of a drink. This river bursts out from within us flowing from our innermost beings to glorify God. John 7: 25-44. In Ezekiel 47: 9 we are told that life flourishes everywhere this water flows. Anyone can come to Jesus and drink to become a river of living water. In Romans 5: 1-2 we have five wonderful grace blessings coming to us all because of what Jesus has done for us.

True and lasting peace with God.

A perfect relationship with God the Father.

Permanent access to God's kindness and grace.

God's righteousness making us flawless in His eyes.

Incredible joy as we anticipate the gift of God's very own glory.

We cannot earn these blessings from God through our own goodness or efforts, they are grace blessings to be received by His children to equip us to know we are sons and daughters with the authority to help others. They are transferred into our accounts with God, through all that Jesus has done for us on the cross. We can relax and enjoy God as Father and enjoy all He has done for us through the blood sacrifice of Jesus Christ our Lord. We need to learn to rest in God and enjoy Him for who He is, as He reveals Himself to us through Jesus and in the Scriptures. In Psalm 91: 1-2, God reveals Himself to us as our shelter, shadow, refuge, place of safety. As we learn to place our trust in Him as all of these wonderful things we can go deeper and deeper into Him and enjoy Him. The remainder of this psalm describes the many promises He makes available to us, His children, when we live in this kind of grace and kindness relationship with Him. His faithful promises are our armour and protection as He covers us, shelters us, rescues us, protects and honours us as His grace children. We do not need to be continuously running about trying to earn God's favour, just concentrate on doing those things He is calling you to do. All that God requires of us is satisfied by the sacrifice of Jesus on the cross. The Christ within you is enough to satisfy God. He is El Shaddai or God the Enough. In writing to Titus, Paul emphasises seven things God has done for us through His kindness and love. Titus 3: 4-7 NLT.

God saves us.

God washes away our sins.

God gives us new birth.

God gives us a new life.

God generously pours out the Spirit on us.

God declares us righteous.

God gives us eternal life.

These seven grace blessings come from God to us because of His mercy through Jesus Christ our Saviour. Why don't you take some time now to thank God for these seven things and worship Him in Spirit and truth, taking time to enjoy Him and all He has done for you child of God. I pray that as you do so the Holy Spirit would fill you as a river of living water and cause God's love to burst its banks with kindness all over you. Why don't you enjoy Him as much as He enjoys you?

I believe that as we learn to enjoy God something of His glory clings to us and can be seen by others and it attracts them to us. They seem to see something supernatural around us which is very attractive, something they long for and hunger for. Religion is described in the Bible as caring for orphans and widows in their distress and not being conformed to the corruption of this world. James 1: 27. There are many orphans and widows in society, falling into this condition spiritually as well as physically and they need our help. We can introduce them to God as Father and the One who wants them as His adopted children. We can do this because this is our own experience of God as Father. True religion in other words is relational and shows people who they are, why they are here, what God wants them to do and where they will go when they die. It is full of hope, joy and abundant life. The world needs these things desperately, so let us release them like a mighty flowing river and show Church the way it was always meant to be, a river of living water.

What will this decade be remembered for? It has begun with a pandemic called corona virus which is shaking the nations in every way. This age is coming to an end to be replaced by the age of the King and His coming Kingdom. Isaiah 24 predicts the judgements of God upon the nations for twisting God's instructions, violating His laws and breaking His everlasting covenants. God will not allow mankind to twist, violate and break His holy Word without the repercussions outlined by the prophet in Isaiah 24-26. The earth is suffering from the sins of the people as a curse consumes it. There is a spirit of anti-Christ gripping the nations at the close of this age and we are called as God's people to pray and stand against it as it rears its ugly head against Israel and the Church.

In Matthew 24 we read about horrible epidemics as being one of the birthing pains associated with the contractions before the Kingdom is birthed out. Jesus has fore warned us that wars, earthquakes, epidemics and famines will ravage the earth in the last days. The breaking apart of the world's godless systems is destined to happen as part of the shaking in Scripture. God's holy people are not to panic or become fearful as these things unfold, we are to endure right to the end. Now that the contractions have begun, they will continue until the birthing of God's Kingdom from out of the womb of the Father. Jesus also spoke about seismic events of epic proportions and we now know that an asteroid is heading on a collision course with the earth around 2029. It is predicted to strike the border between California and Mexico and it could be the size of four football pitches in diameter when it strikes. Such an event could put us back into the dark ages as far as technological advances are concerned, it would cause devastation on a global scale unprecedented by modern man.

To survive and thrive this decade we need to keep God right at the very centre of our lives. We need to know God as Jesus knew Him and serve Him the way Jesus did. We must move forwards as the psalmist prayed in Psalm 86: 11, with loyal, undivided hearts that bring honour to God's Name. Our hearts need to be teachable, full of God's truth, pure and set apart for God and His coming Kingdom. We must keep God on the throne in the very centre of our hearts and not in any way marginalise Him. Our faith is about to be tested like never before and we need to be ready and prepared for all that is about to come. Don't listen to people telling you the Church will be raptured out of all these troubles because they might be wrong, it is best to be prepared for them. 1 John 5: 1-21.

Whenever trouble strikes, I will keep crying out to You, for I know Your help is on the way. God, there is no One like You, there's no other God as famous as You. You outshine all others and Your miracles make it easy to know You. Lord Almighty, you are the One who created all the nations; look at them, they're all on their way. Yes, the day will come when they all will worship You and put Your glory on display. You are the One and only God. What miracles! What wonders! What greatness belongs to You! Teach me more about You, how You work and how You move, so that I can walk onward in Your truth until everything within me brings honour to Your Name. Psalm 86: 7-11 TPT.

The Greek word used for worship in the New Testament is Proskuneo and it means to bow, to kiss, to worship. The angels bow down before Christ and kiss Him in worship and so can we. Hebrews 1: 6. This is most beautiful. Jesus is the complete fullness of deity living in human form. He wants to empower us to further discover the depths of His extravagant love because He is an extravagant lover of His children.

In Genesis 22: 4 we read that Abraham looked up and saw something away into the future. Jesus mentions this in John 8: 56. Jesus is saying that Abraham saw His death and resurrection as he walked towards Mount Moriah or Calvary and this was the same place Abraham was told by God to go and sacrifice his own son Isaac. God was setting the scene for two fathers and two sons and Jesus says that Abraham was filled with delight as he saw this scene before him and Isaac. Abraham would tie his promised son to the altar but then God would intervene and provide a substitute in his place, a ram caught by its horns in a thicket. Abraham saw the Substitute, the Messiah waiting nearby, waiting to be sacrificed rather than the sons of God, no wonder he was filled with delight at what he saw in the Spirit realm that day as they travelled towards the place of sacrifice. When the Spirit of resurrection came on Abraham, he believed that God would raise Isaac from the dead and they would both return from Mount Moriah. Thank God that Abraham looked up and saw on that day because he was looking and seeing into another Father's future involving substitution and resurrection and it filled him with delight.

One of the last things Jesus did before leaving this earth to return to the Father's side was to remove the sandals from His disciple's feet and wash them. John 13: 1-17. By removing their sandals and washing their feet, Jesus was showing them that He was granting them a new inheritance, His own. The sandal is often used in covenants of inheritance in Hebrew culture. Joshua 1: 3. Ruth 4: 1-12. Every defilement would be removed so that they could place the souls of their feet upon the new covenant inheritance. God likewise told Moses to remove his sandals as he was about to receive a new inheritance, the holiness of God and the authority that came with it. Exodus 3: 5. When Christ saves us, He removes every defilement and gives us the authority as sons and daughters to place our feet upon every new covenant inheritance. We have been granted a new inheritance by being washed and seated with Christ in the heavenly realms. We are God's holy, anointed servant-sons with authority here on earth to enforce the terms of His new covenant, the terms of grace, mercy and love. Arise and go as an ambassador for Christ. He has granted you a new covenant inheritance, His own.

In Romans 8: 28-34 we see that God the Father has a destiny plan for each of our lives. We are also told the Jesus prays for us in heaven as our High Priest, Advocate and Mediator. Hebrews 7: 25. The Holy Spirit also prays for us according to Paul in Romans 8, while we are here on the earth. This is wonderful truth because it demonstrates God's commitment to us to all He is calling us to do through His destiny plans. How does God reveal His destiny plan to us? Romans 8: 30 tells us how. Firstly, He calls us to Himself by saving and redeeming our lives. Secondly, He transfers His perfect righteousness into our new lives in Christ. Thirdly, He co-glorifies us with Christ in the heavenly realms. There it is God's destiny plan for each one of us and also His promise in Romans 8: 32 that all the resources of heaven are at our disposal to finish the plan. These wonderful plans were put in place by God before we were even born, they are eternal plans. Even angels gaze into them in wonder as they see God fulfilling them. So, what does all of this mean? It means that God is standing with us and makes all the resources of heaven available to make it happen. It means that God has proved His love for us by giving us His greatest treasure, the gift of His Son. It means that God will give us everything else He has to give to get us across the finishing line. It means that both Jesus and the Holy Spirit are praying for us every day of our lives, which means we can feel secure and strong in the Lord and in His mighty power.

20

INVISIBLE REALMS

I n Luke chapter 16: 19-31, Jesus gives us a teaching to show us the reality of eternal life and heaven and hades. There seems to be a great reluctance to speak about hades these days, as if it isn't politically correct and although the Bible speaks about heaven ten times more than hades, it is a subject we must speak about because it is real. We need to reveal truth and make people aware that our efforts to convince them about Him and what He did for us on the cross are worthwhile. In the story in Luke, Jesus contrasts the life of a rich man and a beggar. The rich man is not named but we are told he wore a purple robe which signified he was surrounded by luxury like a king. The poor beggar is named Lazarus which means "God helps". In all of Jesus' parable stories only Lazarus is ever named. Lazarus dies and is escorted by God's angels into paradise where he is cared for by the father of all who have faith, Abraham. Later, the rich man died but he finds himself in hades in torment. There is a reversal of roles and fortunes here in the story and both men are fully conscious of their past, present and future in a scene described by Jesus where the rich man can see Lazarus and even shout across a huge chasm to speak to him. The rich man describes himself as being in agony in flames of fire, while Lazarus is being comforted in the glory realm. Abraham informs us that it is not possible to cross from hades realm to the glory realm as the chasm between the realms is too huge. Abraham becomes Lazarus' spokesman in the story as he addresses the rich man, reminding him that the choices and decisions he had made on earth had meant he was now in hades for all eternity. The rich man then pleads with Abraham for his five brothers but he is told that the warnings given by Moses and the prophets in the holy Bible is enough to bring them to repentance, so that they can be saved from hades. Abraham is elevating the importance of the Word of God to bring people the revelation needed to be saved and receive God's grace, forgiveness and mercy. He elevates the written words of God above supernatural miracles such as resurrections from the dead.

What do we make of this revelation by Jesus about the afterlife? Firstly, it is very real for every one of us whether we choose to acknowledge it or not. It is the destiny of men to experience eternal life with or without God. Secondly, the choices and decisions we make about God, Jesus and other people really matter because we are held accountable for them. The rich man had opportunity to show love and care to Lazarus when he was laid daily at his gate but he chose to ignore him. The rich man had the resources to help him practically but he chose not to. It is clearly foolish to think we can live in this world selfishly with no regard for others in community. Abraham addresses the rich man as friend expressing God's desire for him throughout his life but the rich man failed to know God as friend, presumably because he was totally consumed by his own extravagant selfish lifestyle. Many people will find this story told by Jesus to be disturbing and very uncomfortable, which is good as it is meant to be. He is trying to waken us up to the realities of eternity and the seriousness of facing God when we die. One thing is for sure, we are all at some point going to die and leave these physical bodies. When that happens, we will still be fully alive in soul and spirit for all eternity. People frequently propose that death is death and oblivion is what follows but Jesus says otherwise. We need to be clear about this so that we can help people to consider their need to open their hearts to God and come to know and experience Him. In John 17: 3, Jesus is praying to the Father and He declares that eternal life means to know and experience You as the only true God, and to know and experience Jesus Christ, as the Son whom You have sent. Eternal death is the opposite of eternal life, death being separation from God eternally, something God never wanted for anybody. In Jesus' story about Lazarus the rich man becomes concerned for the eternal destiny of his brothers because he doesn't want them to experience what he is now experiencing in hades. God reminds him through Abraham that He has left revelation behind in the form of His Word the Bible to help them find Him. It is clear from the rich man's response that he is not that confident that the Bible will be enough for them. My friend, the Holy Bible is God's Word to mankind and the power of God for the salvation of both Jew and Gentile or non-Jew. Romans 1: 16-17. We must read it and pay close attention to what it says beginning with the four gospels and the book of Acts. The whole point of the Bible is to create faith in us to believe in Jesus as the Son of God and our personal Saviour and Lord. Romans 10: 5-11.

God never sends people to hades. People choose themselves to prefer separation from God through unbelief and godlessness in this life and the next. Hades is simply what people choose both here in this life and in the next. Jesus spoke about heaven and hades to give us God's true perspective on the matter and to get us to turn away from sinful living by saying sorry to God and living differently. We can only do this when empowered by the Holy Spirit of God and in obedience to the Word of God. To become a follower of Jesus we have to repent or turn back towards God. We then need to confess our personal shortcomings to Him and receive His forgiveness. By believing in Jesus' sacrifice for us on the cross, we are forgiven and receive new life and new birth through the Holy Spirit. God then declares us righteous by His grace and we can begin to live a new quality of life empowered supernaturally by His Spirit. Titus 3: 3-8. This is God's message to all humanity: to fear God is true wisdom, to forsake evil is real understanding. Job 28: 28. Either we choose to live our lives in the holy fear of God our Righteous Judge and turn away from all evil or we do not, either way we shall reap what we sow. This is one of God's eternal and universal laws which we are all subject to in this life and the next. Some people refuse to acknowledge God's existence preferring to live as they like hoping no consequences will follow. The bible calls this foolishness, Psalm 14: 1-7. Why would God go to all the trouble and agony of sacrificing His only Son and leave us a record of it all in the Bible, His book for nothing? How can the miracle of the nation of Israel be explained if there is no God? Everybody has faith in something but not always in the right thing. There is so much to lose by refusing and rejecting God and His gift of eternal life. Eternal regret can only follow just as it did for the rich man in Jesus' story. I plead with you today as an ambassador for Christ to turn back to God and you will find Him waiting patiently for you. God is your loving, compassionate Father, who pursues you daily with His goodness and love. So why would I fear the future? For Your goodness and love pursue me all the days of my life. Then afterward, when my life is through, I'll return to Your glorious presence to be forever with You. Psalm 23: 6 TPT. God wants to take you to His Menuha or the waters of His resting place. Psalm 23: 1-3. Come now and you will find Him waiting there for you. Psalm 23: 4-5.

The prophet Habakkuk saw God moving and coming in chapter 3. He saw God's brilliant splendour filling the heavens and the earth, it was awesome and powerful as God the Eternal One marched across the land in anger and fury to trample the nations. The prophet is seeing God coming to rescue His chosen people from their oppressors and persecutors. Habakkuk 3: 16. The prophet is determined to rejoice in the Lord even though his circumstances and situation are difficult. What about you, will you honour God by continuing to rejoice in Him despite your circumstances?

Apostle Paul defines the Kingdom of God in Romans 14: 17, as living a life of goodness, peace and joy in the Holy Spirit. There is a kingdom of God lifestyle characterised by goodness, peace and joy in the Holy Spirit available to every believer. It should be the aim of every believer to learn to live such a life. When we do, even in the times of darkness, God's light will shine through us. Our altitude determines our attitude and keeps us joyful in the Sovereign Lord. We look up to God and His Kingdom and place our hope and trust in the Most High our coming King. God has come to save us. We can trust in Him and not be afraid. He is our strength and song. He is giving us the victory.

Isaiah 12: 2. He is holding us up with His victorious right hand. Isaiah 41: 10.

False teachers are being sent to cause divisions and distort the truths of the faith. Every sect has done this since Christ's glorious resurrection and ascension. You can see them today on every street corner and every main thoroughfare in the land. We must be able to vigorously defend and contend for the beliefs passed down to us over the centuries. It is very sad when believers are thrown into chaos and confusion by false teaching. Jesus warned us that in the end times such things would proliferate. Matthew 24: 4 and 11. Jude or Judah was a half-brother of the Lord Jesus and he wrote his short letter to people who could have been living as early as twenty years after the Lord's life, death and resurrection. These false teachers had perverted the message of God's grace into a licence to commit immorality. The end result of this is godless living and total compromise with the unbelieving world. Jude reveals that God will destroy the ungodly, who are guilty of unbelief, those given over to immorality, those who slander heavenly beings which includes God and Jesus as well as the Holy Spirit and finally those corrupting the Church. Did you realise that unbelief is such a serious sin that God will destroy those guilty of it? Jesus speaks about this very clearly in Luke 16: 19-31 as I have already mentioned. Are we acutely aware of this as we share the message of the cross in evangelism? Unbelief is the one thing which people cannot be forgiven for according to Jesus in John 16: 9.

The Church has gone soft on this issue. I don't mean we all need to become hades-fire preachers but we do need to speak clearly to people about the eternal consequences of unbelief. Did you know that Jesus spoke more about hades than about heaven? This one issue is an example of how the world has managed to muzzle the Church through false teaching. How can we expect people to get saved if they don't know what they are being saved from? I meet people regularly on the street who proudly and arrogantly refuse to believe in God and reject the notion that this carries eternal consequences. They have made their choice and chosen a lifestyle promoting it. While they are still alive and

God still has a voice, they can be saved but only through repentance leading to a godly lifestyle.

In 1 John 2: 1-6 and 15-29, John is warning us about talking like believers but not living like believers. He is saying that those who say they live in God, should live their lives as Jesus did. John is telling us to live lives of love for God, one another and the lost. Love will do what is right to please God, bless other believers and warn the unbelievers to repent and turn to God while they still have time. As those who have tasted the grace of God, we can now share it with authority with others because we have a story or testimony to offer them.

Jonah was a reluctant prophet and evangelist, Jonah chapters 1-4. He didn't want the pagans who had made life a misery for God's people repenting and being saved from judgement by God. He had a bit of an attitude problem towards the lost. Amazingly, despite his attitude God used him to share a prophetic message that brought revival to a nation for over one hundred years. Yes, Jonah had a prophetic message because the Hebrew word for overthrown or destroyed is the word Hafak and it also means to be overturned, changed or converted. When Jonah preached- Forty days from now Ninevah will be overthrown, He was also opening the door for grace and mercy and the Ninevites grabbed them joyfully. The same word that signified judgement also signified the possibility of repentance and forgiveness and we have that same prophetic, evangelistic word today. 2 Peter 3: 9. Only God knows how people will respond to His gospel message, we do not we are only sent ones to deliver it, the rest is up to the Holy Spirit. God gave Jonah a life- giving word for the people he sent him to and He will do the same with us. When we daily give ourselves over to Him as living sacrifices, He promises to use us to deliver His gospel message to people He loves and died for.

The Hebrew root word for mercy in the Bible is a plural word. The word for sin is singular which means God's mercies are bigger than any of our sins. There is no sin unforgiveable apart from the sin of dying in unbelief, then it is too late to believe and the sacrifice of Jesus has been rejected forever. In Lamentations 3 we read that God's mercies are new every morning because great is His faithfulness. The Father loves to honour what Jesus paid for us on the cross. God loves to show mercy rather than judgement and this is clearly shown by Jonah's experiences as explained above. Do not allow the devil to lie to you and tell you that you have committed a sin that is too big for God to forgive because that is untrue to His Word, nature and promises. What Jesus did for us on the cross is bigger than any of our sins so receive His forgiveness and also be assured that when God forgives, He also forgets so you and I must try to do the same. Psalm 139. He separates us from our sins as far as east is from west which is an eternal distance as there are no poles there as at north and south. God forgives us in spite of all we have done. Psalm 103: 1-5. He is always ready to forgive because of His kindness and love. Psalm 86: 5-6.

When we come to God for His forgiveness we enter into a Father-Child relationship and can expect His protection all throughout our lives. We see this through His promises in Psalm 91. God provides a throne for us to sit on under the shelter of His Name Shaddai, which means God the Destroyer of Enemies. This is a special place only accessible to the royal children of God purchased by His grace, it is the place of favour reserved for the King's children. As we sit at peace under His mighty shadow no curse or disease can reach us. The wings of the cherubim covering the ark of the covenant on the mercy seat are over us because Hebrews 6 tells us our hope is anchored onto God's heavenly mercy seat. The angelic messengers have special authority to protect us and keep us from stumbling. We can even walk unharmed among the fiercest powers of darkness and trample them under our feet with authority. Psalm 91: 14-16 assures us lovers of God of His protection, safety and security. He promises to answer our prayers for help and to be near to us in times of trouble to comfort and give us His full Yeshua or salvation. Praise God for so many wonderful promises given to us during this time of trouble and tribulation at the beginning of this new decade in 2020. Psalm 91 and Isaiah 12 are to be rocks of faith for us at this time so meditate on them and speak them out as declarations over your life and those you love and care for.

— 21 —

PROPHECY

Jesus is the greatest of all the prophets, so what did He prophesy and how are we to respond?

Jesus unfolds the future in Matthew 24, Luke 21 and Mark 13. We will return to Matthew 24 later but first Joel chapters 1 to 3. Joel tells us that the new age of the Kingdom of God will come when Israel is suffering great economic and oppressive hardship. Joel 1. Four different types of locust have stripped the land bare and Joel tells us that his prophecy ought to be passed down from generation to generation to prepare ourselves for it. Joel 1: 3. The four different types of locust may be different armies invading the land and ruining the economy. At the end of this terrible time in Israel, Jesus returns to earth with His angel armies. Joel calls this the day of the Lord where Jesus delivers the Jewish people, then pours out the Holy Spirit upon them. Joel 2: 28-32. After doing so Jesus then gathers the world's armies together into the valley of Jehoshaphat or the Lord judges to judge them for harming His people, scattering them and dividing up His land. Joel 3: 1-2. Every nation taking up arms against Israel will be included as an enemy nation. This will be a time of war when judgement will be pronounced against many nations. Yeshua or Salvation will deliver the Jews and their God given homeland and bless the land of Israel as He lives alongside them for a period of time. Revelation 19: 11- 20: 6 describes this period after Christ's victorious return

He will rule over the nations from His throne in Jerusalem and we shall reign with Him. How can we be better prepared for the fulfilment of these promises and prophecies? We need to treasure and value each one and pass them on to one another to continually remind each other of the future from God's perspective as written in His Word. There is a danger we may lose sight of this and be deceived if we don't. In Genesis 12: 3 God promises to bless those who bless Israel. We can do this by praying for them and sowing financially into Messianic ministries there if we have the means to do so but we also need to pray for one another and our government, so that we have a biblical perspective around Israel and the end times. Again, I cannot stress strongly enough if we fail to grasp and act on these truths we may well be deceived and led astray by false prophecies and ungodly teaching when this time arrives. This is exactly what Jesus began teaching in Matthew 24: 1-8.

Perhaps you are thinking how can these difficult times be all about Israel, where is the Church? Some people have suggested the Church has been removed or raptured but I think it is much safer to make the decision to stand behind our Jewish family and prepare to be here with them. Jesus' words in Matthew 25 would indicate our need to do this because they are His brothers and sisters and we must treat them as if they were Him. Matthew 24: 9-13 describes the situation today for many believers all over the world as they face persecution and death for their faith in Jesus. We are about to enter a very difficult time where many followers of Jesus will stumble and take offense betraying and hating one another. We are being asked to prepare for betrayal, hatred, false prophets, deception, sin, lawlessness and loss of faith and hope. All of these things are a part of community life for us today if we are being honest. We need to endure right to the very end. Matthew 24: 13.

The end of this age will come when we witness what Daniel prophesied in Daniel 8: 13; 9: 27; 11: 31; 12: 11. Whatever that is it will occur in Jerusalem and concern the Jewish people in particular. Matthew 24: 15-28. It will be lights out on the old order as a new order and glory comes to replace the fading glories of this world. Jesus will appear, His day is coming and we need to be alert, prepared, ready and waiting and watching prayerfully for Him. Matthew 24: 29-31. The fig tree in Scripture always refers to the nation of Israel. Matthew 24: 32. We need to watch Israel very closely to observe all these things taking place. They will show us that our Lord's coming is very close at hand. Matthew 24: 32-35. We must not neglect or ignore bible prophecy because God has given us insights into how we can be prepared for His coming day and the end of the age of man. The time to read the old testament prophets is now alongside Jesus' prophecies in the new. As we read them the Holy Spirit will guide us into the truth. John 16: 13.

When unprecedented events occur in history mankind is forced to evaluate what things are most important to us. We are in the middle of such a time right now due to the covid 19 viral outbreak described as a global pandemic. We are witnessing some remarkable things as medics lay their lives down to care for many sick people and others work tirelessly to keep the rest of the population fed and protected. We have seen the very best and the very worst of humanity during this time. Community is being revived through caring acts of compassion and kindness towards others in need. People are trying everything to stay in communication with loved ones facing social isolation because this is important to them for such a time as this. It is as if God is revealing the soul of the nation and giving us opportunity to fight together and love and value one another like never before. It is a level playing field as the virus attacks people of all ages and genders across every layer of society. We need to stand with our government and civil authorities at this time by listening to them and praying for them and all who are risking their lives to care for us. God has promised to hear and answer our prayers. One thing is certain, the world will never be the same again after the pandemic so let us all pray that God would bring permanent change across the nations, leading many to rediscover faith in Him and trust in His Word the holy Bible.

After His resurrection, Jesus appeared to His followers at least eleven times over a period of forty days and He taught them the mysteries of the coming Kingdom of God. In Acts 1: 6, the disciples ask Jesus a question regarding freedom for Israel and restoration of the Kingdom.

This question still waits to be answered in the Father's perfect timing. Jesus is more concerned with equipping the disciples to be His witnesses all over the world following their coming encounter with the Holy Spirit. The disciples were jumping ahead to the very end while there was still a harvest to be gathered in the present. We must not make the same mistake because we have yet to see and experience a mighty move of God in our generation. The end of this age cannot come until every nation has had a demonstration of the reality of God. Matthew 24: 14. Jesus Himself prophesied this in His teaching on the end times in Matthew 24. What does it mean to have a demonstration of the reality of God? It means God breaking through and revealing Himself through supernatural signs, wonders and miracles leading people to call on Christ to be saved. It means human lives are so touched by the power of God that they are delivered from their past bondages and sin permanently. It means unbelievers become believers and go on to become disciples and multipliers themselves. Matthew 28: 18-20. It means Church community is living in victory and having the maximum effect on one another and the world around us. Acts 2: 42-47.

In Zechariah 4: 14, we have two heavenly beings standing in the court of the Lord. In a court you do not stand unless you're on trial, you're a witness giving evidence or the Judge is about to enter the courtroom. To stand up really means that something is about to happen. The two angels also represent two olive trees, they tell us that a double anointing is coming. God is currently preparing and equipping us for all that is about to occur. It must be done not by human strength or power but by the Spirit says the Lord. God wants to complete and finish what He began at Pentecost almost two thousand years ago because that is when the last days or last age of man began and now it must be brought to a completion for the age of Christ and His Kingdom to reign on the earth for one thousand years. The two heavenly beings are witnesses to what God is about to do and they may be the same two witnesses we read about in Revelation 11: 1-14. Haggai 2: 6 speaks about the Lord shaking the heavens and the earth until we get our priorities right. But He also gives a promise that He will bless His people as we respond to His calling during a time of global shaking of the nations. Something is about to happen that will be global and unprecedented in the spiritual realms and God is preparing us for it now.

Samson is a picture of God's Church community having compromised with the world which caused our eyes to be gouged out but now our hair is beginning to grow back in again. A double anointing is coming to help us finish what began in Acts which is world evangelisation and discipleship. Samson finished what he had begun but he had to die in the process. God gave him supernatural strength for one more act which brought the house of the enemy down. Judges 16: 23-30.

Whatever God is doing in your life right now just hang on in there because it is preparation to be anointed to bring in the harvest. We all have a different part to play but each is just as important there are no superstars in the Body of Christ, we all need one another. Psalm 62 tells us there is no such thing as failure with God because God doesn't ask us to be successful, just faithful. We are called to do what He asks us to and leave the results up to Him. One plants, one sows but God gives the increase. 1 Corinthians 3: 5-7. The remainder of this chapter in 1 Corinthians 3 explains how important it is to God that we each carry out His plan for each one of our lives as Paul explains to us that we are to be involved in teamwork. Don't look at other people and compare yourself, just get on with doing what God is asking you to do because nobody else can. What do you have that you have not received? 1 Corinthians 4: 7. The answer to this rhetorical question is nothing, so all the glory will go to God anyway.

In 1 Samuel 28 we are told that Saul hires a medium to call up Samuel's spirit from the dead. Saul did this because he was about to go into battle with his three sons and men against a huge army and he wanted to know the outcome having failed to hear from God earlier. When God is silent, we continue walking with Him until He speaks, we never ever consult mediums, spiritualists or fortune tellers. Many people are in the habit of doing this today and by doing so they are bringing curses upon themselves and their families by opening doors into the occultic realms. Once opened these doors can only be closed through repentance and the blood of Christ. Saul hears from Samuel that he will be defeated in battle, lose his life and his three sons. He was never meant to have known this ahead of time but it was his own fault because he had disobeyed the word of the Lord in Deuteronomy 18: 9-14 and he knew exactly what he was doing. The woman medium felt sorry for Saul and prepared a meal for him and his two soldiers, it would be their last meal before facing certain death the next morning. This chapter clearly shows us that after death the human spirit leaves the body to rest until the resurrection of the dead. Those who think otherwise are clearly wrong and need to re-think their spirituality.

It also shows us that mediums have access to the spirit realms, which is why God tells us not to use them in order to protect us from harm. How Saul must have deeply regretted his actions that night when he did not get the news he longed for and now he knew the next day was going to be an unmitigated disaster for him, his sons and his men on the battlefield. God tells us to trust in Him with all our hearts because He has a good plan for our lives. Proverbs 3: 5-6. In Numbers 22-24 a Moabite king called Balak hires a medium called Balaam to curse Israel but the medium can only bless the people of God. The king tries everything he knows to bribe him but to no avail. The medium's life is saved by his donkey at one point when God's angel stood in their way. This medium was restricted to speak only blessings over God's chosen people at the risk of his own life. He finds himself caught up in a spiritual battle in the heavenly realms as well as the earthly. If you are reading this having already consulted a medium you can be forgiven and the curse broken off you and your family through the blood of Jesus shed on the cross for you. You must repent by asking God for His forgiveness and promising Him you will never do such a thing again. Thank God for showing you it was wrong and shut the door on the occult in your life and keep it shut.

Believers who have entered the occult also need to repent or they face the danger of being oppressed by demonic spirits. Allow the Holy Spirit to search your heart and shine light on any darkness that may be lingering there. Confess to God anything revealed and declare out loud the power of the blood of Jesus over your life, testimony and family. If you have been struggling with habitual sins, unforgiveness, uncontrollable emotions like anger, fits of rage, negative thoughts and speaking against others it is a sure sign something in your life needs to go whether you are saved or not. Satan will enter through opened doors that give him a foothold in your life if you do not close them forever and keep them closed. I do not believe you can be possessed but you certainly can be oppressed so deal with it now and move on. Psalm 139.

In Ezekiel 47 the prophet is being escorted back and forth across a stream of water until it becomes a river too deep to walk across. This happens four times with a walking distance of 530 metres each time. Every 530 metres the stream became deeper because the man was taking the prophet deeper into God and His plans and purposes. We are being called deeper and deeper into our God so let Him take you and I in much deeper. The further the prophet walked away from the Temple or religion the deeper the water. The prophet now needs a new strategy to get to the other side, he has to swim for the first time because he is out of his depth. He was no longer in control because rivers have strong undercurrents and it would take him where it wanted not necessarily where he wanted. He had to abandon himself to the river and trust he would be taken to the right place at the right time. The river takes him across to the other side over 2000 meters further downstream to a place he had never been before and he saw something remarkable when he looked back. He saw fruit trees that had supernaturally grown all along both sides of the river with a monthly crop and healing leaves. His walk of faith had accomplished something supernatural because he had trusted God and went with the flow of the Holy Spirit. Let God take you in much deeper. Let God take you where He wants you to go. Go with the flow and don't resist it. Get ready for a supernatural move of the Spirit way beyond anything you have yet to experience.

22

F'S STORY

I had a great upbringing with my mom and dad. I had a lot of happy memories until I was 14 when my dad was spiked with drugs and died overnight, which devastated me. I started to rebel against everyone and didn't really care what would happen to me anymore. Before I knew it, I was taking a lot of party drugs and getting into trouble.

When I was 19, I made the worst mistake of my life when I tried a heavier drug for the first time and it seemed to take all my worries away. For the next eleven years I was addicted to heavier drugs. I was a full- blown drug addict searching for a way out, seriously depressed and full of fear. After trying everything for a decade and failing every time, I had accepted that this was my life and I was going to die this way. I just could not see a way out anymore.

In March 18th 2019 I entered the rehab centre still convinced that nothing was going to make me well again. I just kept praying and asking Jesus Christ to help me. I was weak and helpless and needed His help. As the weeks and months went on my life was changing as God showed me His love and the desire for drugs began to go away. I realised I was beginning to think about life completely differently. God showed me He had a plan for my life if I kept making the right choices. For the first time in years, I felt safe and began to feel spiritually strong.

I am 14 months in now and am blown away every time I think about what He has done in my life and I am excited about my future. Now I am able to help other drug addicts and tell them there is another way in life, there is hope for them. Praise God that I have all my family back in my life now. It is great to see them happy. I am looking forward to a happy life with my daughter and family carrying out whatever God has planned for us.

Used by permission from F.

23

END TIMES PSALMS

End times Psalms. In the Hebrew language the Bible titles Psalms 20, 21 and 22 as end times psalms and TPT, The Passion Translation follows this interpretation. So why are they called end times psalms? What insights do they give us into the end times? If you believe we have been living in the end times since Pentecost we need to listen to these three psalms and allow them to prepare us for this coming season.

Psalm 20 is a song of trust in the Lord. Psalm 21 is a celebration of praise to God for His strength and deliverance and Psalm 22 is a prophetic portrait of the cross, resurrection and reign of Jesus following His return to earth. So, there it is in very simple form, we are to trust in the Lord, depend on His supernatural strength and declare the power of His death and resurrection until He returns to rule over the nations. Psalm 22 prophetically describes the sufferings of the cross to verse 21 and from 22 to the end it describes the resurrection and return of Christ. The Holy Spirit anointed David to write these three end times psalms to prepare us for all that is coming even before the New Testament was written. Like many of the Old Testament prophets David was given a revelation of the end times. It is important to read all three psalms together to get a tremendous sense of Christ's victory through His suffering, death, resurrection and glorious return to rule the nations. His victory is our victory as we suffer with Him and reign with Him at His coming. We are His spiritual seed, serving Him and declaring His wonders to future generations, who will glorify Him until at last it is finished.

In Psalm 20 we see the end times will be days of danger causing us to depend on the Lord for His deliverance, safety, support and supernatural help. We will be in a spiritual battle for the souls of men. We will know great answers to prayer as miracles manifest. We will rise up full of courage to enforce the victory of Jesus Christ all over the nations. In Psalm 21, we will be strong in the strength of our King. We will pursue His heart's desires. We will enjoy rich encounters with Him full of resurrection power. We will experience His forever-love holding us firm. We will see His victory over those opposing Him as He puts His might on display. We will sing and praise His glorious power. In Psalm 22, as we preach and teach the blood of the cross, we will share in the sufferings of our King but also in His resurrection power. We will need to endure by trusting in God for His deliverance. We will gather together as lovers of Yahweh to praise and glorify Him as He responds to our sufferings. The poor and broken will come and eat until satisfied. People will remember and return to the Lord from the four corners of the earth. Every nation will come and worship Him as He returns to take charge of all the nations. All will worship this worthy King. This teaching is more familiar to us in Matthew 24, Luke 21, Mark 13, 1 Timothy 4 and 2 Timothy 3 but here it is much earlier on in these three psalms written by David under the inspiration of the Holy Spirit the true Author of the Holy Bible.

Isaiah the prophet takes us the same theme in chapter 2: 1-4. He is given a vision of the last days where he sees people from all over the world streaming to God's House on Mount Zion to worship. He also sees a great hunger and thirst for God among the nations as international disputes are settled and peace becomes the norm rather than war. It is the Lord Himself who mediates between the nations as the Tsar Shalom or Prince of Peace. Isaiah 9: 2-7. Ezekiel predicts defeat for the enemy nations attacking Israel and a restoration for God's covenant people as He displays His holiness among them for all the nations to see. Ezekiel 38 and 39. Daniel is given a vision of the time of the end in Daniel 12. In his vision Daniel also sees Israel at the heart of the action experiencing great anguish but also resurrection glory. Daniel is told that many will rush here and there, and knowledge will increase. Israel will suffer tribulation for three and a half years before deliverance comes through their Messiah's return. Joel sees the judgements against every nation who has harmed the Jewish people, scattered them among the nations and divided up God's land. Joel 3: 1-3. The nations responsible are called to arms into the valley of Jehoshaphat where God will pronounce judgement upon them. Amos sees a promise of restoration for the house of David as God returns the exiles to Israel to rebuild the ruined cities and restore the land. Amos 9: 11-15. Obadiah sees a day when all godless nations will be judged for what they have done to Israel. Obadiah 15-21. Micah sees the Lord's future reign in the same vein as Isaiah in Micah 4: 1-5 but he also sees the exiles returning and the kingship restored to Jerusalem. Micah 4: 6-13. Habakkuk sees a vision of the returning King of glory that makes him shake with terror and quiver with fear. Habakkuk 3. He sees the earth shaking and the nations trembling as His awesome power is revealed. He also sees disaster for the nations who invade Israel. Zephaniah sees the Lord restoring Israel before all the nations of the earth as He gathers them together to bring them home again to their promised land to dwell there forever under the blessing of their Messiah. Zephaniah 3. Zechariah sees the Lord restoring His people at the return of their King and Messiah. He sees the future deliverance of Jerusalem and restoration of God's people to their land when the Lord Himself fights for His people and delivers them through supernatural signs, wonders and miracles. He sees all nations coming to Jerusalem to worship the King. Zechariah 9 to 14. Malachi sees the coming day of judgement when the Son of Righteousness will rise with healing in His wings. He also sees the coming of John the Baptist in the Spirit of Elijah to proclaim the Messiah's first coming and prepare the hearts of the people to believe in Him. Clearly, God has been speaking to us through many different prophets about the end times to prepare us for them. There is a consistent witness and testimony in the Word of God that equips us for the time by warning us and giving us foreknowledge on how we can walk with Christ through them. I know some believers believe at some point the Church will be raptured during the tribulation period but others believe it may not occur until half way through or even at the end. I think it is better to be prepared for the end and leave the true rapture up to God as it is His surprise for us. Whenever it occurs it will be just at the right time so let us be well prepared to endure and serve Christ right to the end.

When Yeshua does return it is described in Isaiah 11 and 12 as a wonderful day. He will come anointed by the seven-fold Holy Spirit of Revelation 1: 4 and Isaiah 11: 2. He is coming as the Spirit of the Lord. The Spirit of wisdom, understanding, counsel, might, knowledge and the fear of the Lord. He will usher in an era of great peace globally because He will be a banner of salvation to all the world as all the nations rally to Him. Isaiah 11: 10. He will bring Jewish people home to Israel from all across the nations as they return to celebrate Him. At present only about 50% of Jewish people live in Israel so many more will return. With joy they will drink deeply from the fountain of salvation, Yeshua Himself. With just one breath from His mouth, He will destroy the wicked as He gives justice to the poor and makes fair decisions for the exploited. The earth is going to shake at the force of His Word. Isaiah 11: 4. He will wear righteousness like a belt and truth like an undergarment. Isaiah 11: 5. From Jerusalem the Messiah will rule over both Jews and Gentiles while God's Name is praised all across the nations with great joy because of His majesty, might and greatness. This will be a wonderful day for all of these wonderful reasons.

Although that wonderful day seems very distant it can all happen in one of God's suddenly moments. We see this clearly in Ezekiel 37: 1-14. The Spirit of the Lord takes the prophet to a place of death, into a valley full of dried- up bones scattered everywhere. They were people once alive but now scattered just like the children of Israel. God is inviting the prophet to participate in a miracle. God could do it Himself but He does not want to, He wants to do the miracle in partnership with His prophet. It was a hopeless scene before the prophet but not to God. To God it was an opportunity for a miracle. This scene reminds me of the spiritual and moral state of the nation right now. Unusually, the supernatural transformation would occur immediately with no time gap in between because it would be one of God's suddenly moments. The words spoken by the prophet would become reality immediately. Suddenly dried- up bones come together, stand up and become a great army. Where are the prophets willing to speak with authority to create Gods suddenly moments? This shows us that any hopeless situation is just ripe for a miracle. Is there anything more dead and hopeless than a valley floor full of dried- up scattered bones? What is the most hopeless situation in your life right now because it is ripe for a miracle? The valley had been there for some time looking cursed, unclean, unattractive to all but hungry wild animals. It was in a place like this that God chooses to partner with His prophet to do a miracle. The nation can be transformed by one of God's suddenly moments as we choose to prophesy over it.

The first time the prophet spoke only one half of the miracle occurred as the bones came together with human flesh but without breath, so he was now looking at dead bodies rather than dead bones. The whole miracle could not occur without breath from the four winds. The prophet had to command the four winds to release their breath into the dead bodies so they could live again. The miracle is now complete as a valley of dried- up bones is standing before him like a resurrected army. God is working through the prophet to show him that there is hope for the scattered covenant people of God. They will be gathered together from exile and brought back to the land of Israel through Aliyah something happening today since 1948 when Israel became a nation again. It is a wonderful miracle sign from God that we are living in the last days as we see right before our eyes the miracle that is Israel. Don't miss the miracle because it is opening the door to the return of the Messiah for Isaiah 11 and 12 to occur.

So, what is the day of the Lord in Scripture and how can we be prepared for it? It is the day of God's judgement. Jeremiah 30: 7-9; Joel 1: 15; 2:1-2; Amos 5: 18; Zechariah 1: 14-21 and 14: 1-9; 2Thessalonians 2: 1-12. Before that day comes there will be an apostasy, abandonment or falling away from faith in God, which is what we see happening here in the nation and all over the nations. The apostasy may also involve the establishing of a false global religion, which is really the worship of Satan and not the God of the Bible. God will only allow this situation for a limited time before intervening as He did in Genesis 19: 1-29. What occurred here in Genesis is a biblical pattern or first mention of what is yet to come. The judgements in Exodus are also a part of this biblical first mention and pattern of what is to come as revealed in the book of Revelation. God will judge nations, governments and individuals according to our relationship with Jesus Christ and our treatment of Israel, His covenant people. Matthew 25: 1-46. Joel 3: 1-3. Genesis 12: 1-3.

To be saved by God means to be saved from His judgement through the blood of His Son, Jesus Christ. There is no other way to be saved because this is God's Way not mans. Acts 4: 12. John 14: 1-6. Believers who walk with God will be rewarded according to their obedience as a result of love for God here on earth. 1 Thessalonians 1: 10; 2 Corinthians 5: 10; Hebrews 9: 27-28. Jesus speaks about the conditions here on earth prior to the day of the Lord in detail in Matthew 24 and it will be a very difficult time requiring endurance from the people of God. We should meditate on this passage alongside Matthew 25 regularly to prepare ourselves for the coming day of the Lord. Luke 21 also prepares us for all that is coming and also encourages us to pray that we might be strong enough to escape the coming horrors and stand before the Son of Man. Luke 21: 34-36. For the children of God, the time leading up to the day of the Lord will be very difficult but the day itself will be a wonderful day full of promise and restoration. Isaiah 11 and 12; Isaiah 66: 10-24; 1 Peter 1: 1-9. God's judgement will be a judgement against Satan and all who refuse to embrace Christ's righteousness. Sin entered humanity through Adam but righteousness entered through Christ so judgement is related to all who refuse the embrace of Christ's righteousness. John 16: 7-11.

We are living in some of the most difficult but exciting days because the final portion of prophecies in the Bible are being fulfilled before our eyes. In 1 Kings 3: 1-15, God speaks to Solomon in a dream and asks him a question that is really wonderful. What do you want? Ask, and I will give it to you? What would you ask for if God spoke to you this way in a dream? Solomon asks God for wisdom so that he can govern

God's people well and make wise decisions for them. He wanted a gift from God to benefit others, rather than himself. God was pleased with Solomon's request because it was others centred and unselfish, it was beneficial to the high calling God had placed on his life, the calling of kingship. What gifts do you need to fulfil the calling God has placed on your life? God will give you all you need for everything He is calling you to accomplish for His Kingdom.

The New Testament speaks about heaven ten times more than about hades. John the Immerser's message was turn your life around and come back to the holy God. He then promised that Yeshua would baptise us in the raging fire of the Holy Spirit. We can be engulfed but not burn up like the bush in Exodus 3. God wants to call people to Himself through us by setting us ablaze with His Spirit. This is a fire of attraction, not destruction. It is a fire that draws before it consumes, a most wonderful life-giving thing sent from God to bless His people from heaven. It is a fire that furnishes and equips the people of God to minister to others in the fullness of the power of God. We have yet to receive the fullness of this promise but the fire is coming. Like Solomon I had a dream and this is what God said to me three times, the fire is coming. In 1 Peter 1, Peter is speaking about the day of the Lord or the day when Jesus Christ is revealed to the whole world. See, Isaiah 2: 1-4; Joel 2 and 3; Zechariah 13 and 14. On that day, those who are born again, will receive our priceless inheritance, kept in heaven for us from the Lord. This will be the fulfilment of our salvation or the final part of our soul's salvation. 1 Peter 1: 9-12. God is protecting this for us now in heaven until that day comes. Although we may have to endure many trials until that day comes, we are to remain strong in our faith, because our faith brings us much praise, glory and honour on that great and wonderful day. It will be a day of full revelation for everybody in all the world. 1 Peter 1: 13. He calls us to live as holy, obedient children until it comes. Our Father has no favourites so we are to live in the fear of Him until that day arrives. We are paid for by the ransom price of the blood of the Lamb so we must live like we are ransomed and redeemed. The source of our new, eternal lives is the eternal, living, word of God. The Gospel message is the eternal, living, word of God.

24

THE MAGNIFICENT SEVEN

Revelation 8: 2 is speaking about the magnificent seven Archangels who stand before God with trumpets waiting for His command to blow them. We know from Scripture that Gabriel and Michael are two of these wonderful angelic servants of the Lord. At the sound of each trumpet different judgements are released from heaven to earth during the last days. The final three trumpets contain warnings of great terror for all refusing to repent and turn to God. Some people will face torture for five months by locust-like creatures with painful stings in their tails. After this, four angels lead an army of 200 million troops who kill one third of all the people on the earth. Despite all this suffering people will continue to refuse to repent and turn to God rather than the worship of idols and demons. God's two witnesses appear in between the blowing of the sixth and seventh trumpets. They must complete their testimony to the whole world before the seventh angel can blow his final trumpet, which ushers in the return of the Lord Jesus Christ. Right up to the very end God is giving people opportunity to turn back to Him. It is very difficult to understand why people will continue to reject God's offer of eternal life and choose to continue practicing murder, witchcraft, sexual immorality and theft. This must break God's heart as it was never His intention for mankind.

In Jude 25 we learn that God created time but before doing so there was the ages of eternity. Time will end one day and be overtaken again by the ages of eternity. Time is a temporary part of God's eternal perspective. It is a very small part of a much bigger picture. When the age of man comes to an end it will be overwhelmed by the age of the Messiah. The age of the Messiah will reign for at least one thousand years, Revelation 20: 1-3. This will be one thousand years of resurrection life on earth for faithful believers once dead, now brought back to life again to reign alongside their Messiah. Perhaps they are the faithful ones who died for their faith during the time known as the great tribulation. Blessed and holy are those who share in the first resurrection to reign with Messiah for one thousand years. The remainder of all believers will continue resting in Christ in glory until this set time ends. During this period there will be no Satanic deception or evil influences on earth because Messiah and His priests have conquered the earth. This means two very separate resurrections with one thousand years in between. Why will God allow Satan to be released after one thousand years of imprisonment to deceive the nations again? There is no obvious reason given in Scripture, this is one of God's mysterious things. Deuteronomy 28: 28. Jerusalem and the people of God will be surrounded by Satan's vast armies until God intervenes and fire comes down from heaven and consumes them. Satan will then join the other members of the false or counterfeit trinity in the lake of fire, the false prophet and the beast. Following this all the dead will be judged including death and the grave itself. This is called the second death.

How do you know if your name is recorded in the Book of Life? Only when we repent from our sins, turn back to God by receiving His forgiveness through Christ's blood sacrifice and then live by faith can we be saved from the coming wrath of God. Every name written in the Book of Life is written with the Lamb's precious, sinless blood. Following this final judgement God will create a new heaven and earth without any sea and a new Jerusalem will descend from heaven onto earth and God Himself will live among us. Revelation 21. This new Jerusalem will be a beautiful place of worship free from every curse where God and His people enjoy one another forever. Revelation 22: 1-5. Heaven and earth will no longer be separated but will be one continuous realm accessible to all. In Revelation 22: 20, Jesus promises to come soon or suddenly. We must remain faithful until He comes or He calls us home. Soon is much sooner now than then. We know that the nation of Israel is the fig tree to watch carefully in the last days because when Israel signs a peace treaty, around half way through, things will turn really nasty as the age of men comes to an end. Revelation 12 and 13. Most of John's revelation describes the conditions on earth and God's response throughout this final time period. until He comes.

So, we are marked by love and captured by grace. God marked out our destiny beforehand, He marked us with His love and set us apart to be His children, even before He created this natural world. When did He do this, I hear you saying? At some point in the past, in the supernatural, spiritual realm we were with Him as He embroidered us. Psalm 139: 15-16. At that point God allocated us a specific number of days and recorded them in His book of life in heaven. God's love is a marking love as He marks us as His own. He comes to capture us by His grace because of His love and destiny plans for us. A meditation on Psalm 139 in the Passion Translation may bring this out for you alongside Ephesians chapter 1. Psalm 23: 6 also states that after we die, we return to His glorious presence, which suggests we have already been there.

In Leviticus 6: 13 we are told to keep the fire on our altars burning and don't let it go out. There is nothing sadder than a church community where the fire has gone out. In Revelation 2: 1-7, Jesus gives us the answer to this problem. The church in Ephesus had lost their first love for Christ and one another, their fire had gone out. They are told to repent or the effectiveness of their witness would end because a bad witness is worse than none at all. This word is given to the community in Ephesus, believers who had received the great revelatory epistle from Apostle Paul and yet here they are on the brink of extinction. What had gone wrong? Jesus is warning them that they will lose their place of influence in the Kingdom of God and in their community if they don't repent and return to their passion for Him and one another. Passion for Jesus is the greatest of all motivations. We must seek to have a passionate burning fire for Christ on our altars. The believers in Ephesus had an impressive spiritual CV. They had worked hard and persevered, they didn't tolerate evil, had used spiritual discernment in choosing leadership, had endured trials and persecutions and yet all of this paled into insignificance compared to love for Christ Himself. It almost seems unfair of Jesus to criticize such a community but He does and calls them back to Himself through repentance. They were continuing to function but without the spark of passionate love. They had lost the spark that causes the fire to burn and blaze.

This is a sobering, fearful word from God for all of His people. Our fire can go out and we may not even be aware of it as we carry on regardless. I read scriptures like this and can become really discouraged until I remember 1 Thessalonians 5: 23-24. God wants to make us holy in every way. He works in us until Christ returns to complete us. God is faithful and will never abandon us and He makes things happen because of His faithfulness to us. We are marked by love and captured by grace. Thank God for the dunamis or dynamic power of the Holy Spirit to change and make good where we are cold and damp. In 2 Corinthians 5: 9 we are told that it is our goal to please the Lord. How can we live lives pleasing to the Lord? By living our lives with Him. Even when we depart from our physical bodies and go home to be with the Lord, we still want to please Him, that will never change. We will meet with Christ as soon as we leave these bodies and stand before Him to be judged. He alone is Saviour and Judge of all mankind. He saves us from the wrath of God against the sin of rejecting Christ's sacrifice for us on the cross but we are all held accountable for what we do in our human bodies. 2 Corinthians 5: 1-10. This is an inescapable fact for every single human being who has lived on this earth. After our death comes a standing judgement. Hebrews 9: 27. It is a part of human destiny to be judged by our Creator and Redeemer. Christ the Judge is the one met by John the Apostle on the island of Patmos in Revelation 1. John had never encountered Jesus this way before. His eyes were like flames of fire. A sharp two-edged sword came from His mouth. His face was like the sun in all its brilliance. Revelation 1: 12-16. When John saw Him as Judge, he fell at His feet like a dead man and was only revived when touched by His right hand of grace and mercy.

Like us, John was an imperfect man in need of the grace of God so that he could finish his work and write down the revelation God was giving him. God uses imperfect people like us because He is a God of love and grace who fills us with hope. When our goal is to please Him, He will give us the grace to finish whatever He is asking of us. We need to keep the fire on the altar burning and not allow it to go out. Many will come with pails of cold water and throw them on your altar in an attempt to put your fire out but don't let them do it, stay well away from them even if they claim to be good, well- intentioned people. When God sets you and I ablaze we must stay ablaze and do everything possible to completely finish the work He has asked us to do. People will misunderstand you and question your sanity because they don't have your personal revelation but stay strong and do it anyway and God will bless you. When your time comes to stand before the judgement seat of Christ you will receive your reward through obedience to Him, whether other people agree with you or not. Not everything God asks of us seems to make sense but that is not the point. The cross didn't seem to make any sense at all to the first believers until the resurrection three days later. It is better to try and even fail in obedience to God rather than not try at all and be full of regret. Isaiah 41: 10. Try by faith and leave the outcome to God. I remember when I first heard God telling me to get out and start blessing the homeless, some people thought I was mad but by the grace of God I did it anyway and what blessing has followed. God knows what He is doing and He wants to share His blessings with us no matter how daft it may seem to be. Follow your instinct as led by the Holy Spirit and just get on with it and God will turn up and bless you.

Apostle Peter chooses the third chapter of his second letter to speak about the last days. He tells us not to behave like dogs or washed pigs by becoming caught up again in the corruptions of the world system God has saved us from. He warns us against deceivers, who will question the Messiah's second coming and he goes on to tell us that the world systems are being prepared to be judged by God's fire which will burn them up like a pile of dry hay. However, this will be a day taking everyone living in the world by surprise which suggests all believers have been removed or raptured. The heavenly elements created by God will melt away as God dismantles everything of the present order to establish His new order. The Church has the ability to speed up or slow down this process according to Peter. After this coming day Isaiah 65: 17 and 66: 22 will be the new reality. May we all fulfil the Great Commission to speed up this coming day. Matthew 28: 19-20. Matthew 24: 14. We have the privilege of partnering with the Holy Spirit to make this happen.

So where does passion and motivation come from for God and spiritual realities? Paul the Apostle speaks about this in 2 Corinthians 5: 1-21. If you spend some time meditating on this wonderful chapter you will notice seven major motivations and passions fuelling our service for Christ. The first is mentioned in verse 5 and it is the Holy Spirit. He is our engagement ring, pledge and down payment guaranteeing our full inheritance from God. Developing a relationship with the Holy Spirit is a great joy as He comes to live in us and anoint us for service. Our whole bodies become His holy temple as we learn to hand them over to Him daily. As we get to know Him intimately, we become all the more assured of our heavenly calling and destiny. We need to learn to listen to Him, obey Him and partner with Him and the angels just like Philip in Acts 8.

Secondly, we live by faith not sight which means we carry on doing everything God calls us to do whether we see blessing or not. We see this in verse 7. The Holy Spirit and faith working together are powerful passions and motivators as we obey the word of God. Thirdly, we have the promise that soon we will leave our present bodies behind and go home to be with the Lord, verse 8. This truth produces a joyful confidence in us helping to motivate everything we do. Our heavenly bodies will be our new house built by God Himself, immortal, indestructible, spiritual and powerful. Fourthly, we now live lives pleasing to Him as we find out what pleases our holy God. Our priorities will change as God reveals His destiny plans for each one of our lives, verse 9. Fifthly, we know that we have a soon coming appointment with Christ at His judgement seat, not to face judgement but to receive rewards for obedience for what we have done in these bodies. 2 Corinthians 5: 10. We cannot face judgement for our sins as Christ paid the penalty for us when we believed in Him so there will be no rejection or punishment here for believers as we are scrutinized for rewards.

The sixth thing which motivates and gives passion is a deep awe and respectful fear of the Lord, verse 11. As we get to know Him, we are constantly learning all the more about how magnificent He is, there is none like Him. As we look at the cross and see how much He has done for us there it ought to fill us with a deep respect and fearfulness as we stand in awe of Him. Finally, the seventh motivator is Christ's endless love for us, verse 14. Paul writes about this passionately in Ephesians 3: 14-21 as he describes the wonder of Christ's love for us, he is almost lost for words good enough to describe it. Seven great passions and motivators to meditate upon and fuel our continuing walk with God, Holy Spirit, Faith, Eternal Destiny, Pleasing to Him, Appointment with Him, Awe, Fear and Respect for Him, Christ's endless, dependable love for us. I hope you will take time to meditate on these things and allow the Holy Spirit to fill you with greater levels of passion and motivation for God as you serve Him by faith, wherever He calls you to go. Here is a poem to end this chapter:

Covid 19,
One of the worse things ever seen,
Like a very, very bad dream
Hunting us down in the darkness.

Covid 19, who can forget,
Waking up coughing in a cold sweat,
Endless anxiety all through the day,
Have I or haven't I, will it just go away?

THE FIRE IS COMING

Covid 19,
The old, the young, the in between,
Invisible killer that cannot be seen,
Locking us down in the darkness.

Covid 19,
Fear and terror to the extreme,
Doctors, nurses and carers work as a team,
Keeping us safe in the darkness.

Covid 19,
Changing the nations, changing our lives,
May we all honour those who have passed,
Ultimate sacrifice from first to last.

Covid 19,
Grannies and grandads, moms and dads,
Brothers, sisters, uncles and aunts,
Some bodies loved one, some bodies loss.

Covid 19, has touched every one of us,
Lockdown, distancing, washing our hands,
Painful isolation from those we love,
All throughout our lands.

Covid 19, won't just go away,
We need to be wise and do as they say,
We need to think hard, need to think other,
To treat one another, like sister and brother.

Covid 19, has no authority here,
The blood of the cross keeps us free from all fear,
Living or dying whatever may come,
Our trust is in Jesus, God's glorious Son.

25

ZANDER'S STORY

Hi I am Zander. My parents worked really hard to put food on the table when I was a young lad but my father was an alcoholic ever since he came home from the army and couldn't talk about what had happened to him. I think it is called PTSD today but then it was not recognised so he got little help apart from going to dry out now and then. My dad was a welder to trade and often worked away from home so we never saw him for weeks on end then when he got home, he was drunk most of the time which caused arguments in the house, which often became violent with things getting smashed. We never enjoyed family holidays as we never had the money so I started stealing money and things at a very young age for sweets and little toys to play with. I stole money in primary four and got belted really badly by the head teacher for it but it failed to stop me.

Looking back, I think not seeing my dad or really getting to know him and with all the fighting in the house I felt very unloved and insecure and at that time I was an only child. Dad showed me little love and gave me no attention unless he was drunk and sometimes, he took friends home with him who just wanted to fight with me all the time so I began to stay out of his way and out of the house as much as possible. It helped that my bedroom was on the front door side of the house so

I could sneak out at any time day or night without anyone knowing. I started stealing from shops and also breaking into local houses for more money and had a juvenile record by the time I was thirteen. My friends then introduced me to LSD and I was no stranger to alcohol so most weekends were taken up with one or the other. I was desperately unhappy and began stealing books from the local library to read about witchcraft and the supernatural in an effort to discover who I really was but this never seemed to help.

I was thrown out of the Boys Brigade for bad behaviour but took my New Testament with me and along with the witchy books I began to read it as well. I remember one night coming home really unhappy after swallowing many Valium pills and reading in the book of Acts, about the story of Stephen the first martyr and I couldn't understand why he had died so willingly it really spoke into my heart and also made me angry as he had done nothing to deserve his death. I asked if God was there and real please help me to find You. The stealing and bad behaviour continued to the point where near the end of year 3 in Secondary my head teacher called me in and threatened to expel me from school saying I should now go to an approved school and this really bothered me a lot. I was out walking some three weeks later during the school summer holidays when two young people stopped me in the street and told me about Jesus and the cross and shared their stories with me. I remembered my prayer to God as they were talking and it suddenly occurred that He was real and cared about me because they had come to help me to find him by sharing their stories with me. I met them and their friends a couple of days later and asked Jesus Christ into my life repenting from my sins and what love and acceptance I felt that night, I walked home on cloud nine without the acid, I was high on the love of God and it felt amazing. It was difficult breaking friendships with some of my old pals and it took some time but eventually I did to stop bad behaviours but this left me quite lonely.

I went back to secondary and settled down and there was an immediate improvement. I started to work hard at school, stay away from trouble and found I was good at sports and soon excelled at soccer and running becoming school champion for my year group and scoring many goals at football. I began to feel better about myself and grew in confidence slowly although I had hurt a lot of people and had to work hard at convincing them I had really changed. I eventually became a prefect in year 5 and school boy captain in year 6. I think the head teacher had put the fear of God into me and I thank him for that. Now my biggest struggle was in relationships and this would go on for some time until I left my home town to do further studies somewhere new. I began to read the Bible seriously and meet with others to pray and that really helped me. I can honestly say that God is now the Father I had always wanted because He loves me and wants to share life with me. Thanks for listening to my story and I hope it really helps you to connect with God, love Zander. Zander's story is used by permission.

— 26 —

JABEZ 1 CHRONICLES 4: 9-10

J abez had a difficult start in life much like many of the people sharing their personal stories in this book. His name means he will cause pain or distress because his mother had birthed him in great pain, perhaps as a result of a difficult childbirth. He was labelled from the womb but he rose up to shake off his earthly identity and became more honourable than his brothers. At some point in his life Jabez began to call on God and broke through into a new identity, something we all need to do. Only God the Father gives us our heavenly identity, our true identity in Christ.

In his prayer, Jabez asked God to undo his old label and give him a new one. He wanted every negative, ungodly declaration spoken over him to be reversed and cancelled out. He shows us that no matter what people around us may say or how we are labelled, God is able and willing to turn things around and bless us. The world wants us down and out but God wants us to be blessed and a blessing to others. Jabez wanted to conquer new territory under God's blessing. He was determined not to let his name determine his future. He realised that God had a purpose for both Israel and him and that His purpose is to bless. God has left a record of this in Scripture to encourage us all to follow the example of Jabez. Perhaps like me you had negative things spoken over you by people in authority throughout your life, damaging your confidence and self- esteem. Perhaps Jabez's mother may have seen that her son had a bleak future, with his life full of sorrows and pain. He dealt with this by becoming a man of fervent prayer who knew God and came close to Him.

When Jabez asked God to bless him, he was asking for good relationships, peace of mind, a compassionate heart, a gentle posture and a kindly spirit. He was also asking God to make an impact through his life for the Kingdom of God because he wanted his inheritance. What about you, do you want your inheritance? Jabez wanted the hand of God to bless every part of his life on his journey of faith. He wanted the hand of God to lead and guide him continually. He had a relationship with God and he knew God, so he knew he could be bold with God because God had dreams for his life. Ephesians 2: 10. He had confidence before God in prayer believing Him for big things and so should we.

Jabez is asking God to be with him as He enlarges his territory in the land of Canaan, a territory full of giants. He was ready to fight to inherit his promises because he knew he would have to it wasn't going to be easy. He was ready to fight the good fight, keep the faith, finish the race set before him to inherit his promises. Like Jabez we need to grab the promises of God and act upon them in order to inherit them by faith as we journey on with Him. Just like Jabez, God will grant us our requests because He is a good Father with an intense love for us. In 1 Corinthians 13 the love of God described is a burning, fiery love which sets on fire. It comes from the inner depths of His heart powerfully binding us to Him and to other believers. It is an intense affection that must be demonstrated. It is loyal, endless and unconditional. It is full of feeling and emotion, demonstrated by actions of kindness and compassion. It is the highest form of love. It is the love of the Father, Son and Holy Spirit for one another and their children in heaven and on earth.

We are called to learn to love just like this and it is our highest calling. This kind of love does not come naturally, it must be learned and practiced in our walk with God. It remains long after everything else is finished and forgotten. It will eventually give us understanding of everything and is the beautiful prize for which we run. It is one of the questions Jesus may ask us when we stand before Him. Did you learn to love? Has God's burning, fiery love set us on fire? The fire of God's love is coming, a baptism in fiery love that will transform us if we are willing to receive it.

Jabez had been touched by the love of God and he was emboldened to approach Him and ask Him for more. Like David in Psalm 63, he wanted to come into God's sanctuary presence and drink in more of His power and glory. He knew there was more and he wanted more. He knew God would not deny him for wanting more. What about you? Do you find yourself wanting more of God and His blessings? Jabez shows us this is a good thing and will be well rewarded.

Jabez demonstrates faith, hope and love all working together in his relationship with God. It is quite possible that he was born with some form of disability due to a difficult childbirth, we are not told this. Perhaps this was why his mother saw a life of pain and distress ahead for him. Jabez was determined not to allow any disability to deny him his inheritance. He knew that with God, all things are possible. He had discovered the grace of God at work in his human weakness. 2 Corinthians 12: 9-10. For when I am weak, then I am strong. He knew that God had a plan for his life and it was a good plan, a blessed plan, a plan full of hope, promise and inheritance. Jabez shows us how to relate to God. He was grateful to God, approaching Him with respect, using the word please and this tells us much about him. He had a humble attitude before God, an attitude of gratitude.

God doesn't owe us anything, rather we owe Him absolutely everything. He is gracious and merciful so He spares us from what we deserve and gives us what we don't deserve. In one sense, we are all born with a disability because sin disables and separates us from God and His plans for our lives. Until we allow God's grace and forgiveness to wash our sins away and continue to be washed under the water of His Word, we will remain disabled spiritually. Thank God for the healing blood of Jesus shed for us all on the cross, to heal every kind of spiritual, mental and physical disability. He forgives all our sins and heals all our diseases. Psalm 103: 3. Through sinful human nature we struggle with limitations affecting confidence, self-esteem and identity. People can be better at telling us what we cannot do, than what we can. God tells us we can do all things through Jesus Christ who gives us His strength. Philippians 4: 13. All things means everything with no limitations. God is removing our limitations and replacing them with expectations. Jabez had optimism with a plan, he was a descendant of Judah from the tribe of David, the tribe of the Messianic seed line. He had been born into great expectations from God with a plan for his life free from human limitations, labels and disabilities.

He was God's poetry and masterpiece so that he could do the good things planned for him long ago. Ephesians 2: 10. God's hand was upon his life to impart a blessing to him and God had gone before him to prepare the way and was following on behind him to protect him from the harm of his past. Psalm 139: 5 TPT. This is as true for you and me so be encouraged and step out into God's plans for your life. See yourself as God sees you and throw off all limitations by speaking out loud the promises of God over your life and expectations. If you practice doing this you will be speaking destiny truth over yourself and your loved ones. Remember, God's mighty power is at work in you to accomplish all this. He will achieve infinitely more than your greatest request, your most unbelievable dream, exceeding your wildest imagination! He will outdo them all, for His miraculous power constantly energises you. Ephesians 3: 20 TPT.

I think Jabez knew what it meant to have a broken, repentant heart before God after the pattern of David in Psalm 51. There was something about his attitude that attracted the favour of God to him. Attitude is important to God. The world pushes equality and human rights but Christ humbled, emptied and reduced Himself to come here as God's servant. He gave up His divine privileges to take human form and serve, He came from the highest heights to the lowest depths to serve the plans and purposes of the Father for the human race. Obedience to God always demands a humble attitude to place His will before our own. As a result of His humble attitude Christ now sits in the place of highest honour with the Name above all others. Jabez approached God with a humble attitude, making him more honourable than his brothers and God rewarded him for it. We need to think about this and make it a priority to serve one another in the Body of Christ because this is our highest calling after loving God. Love for one another is a most powerful witness to a very selfish world. For God is working in us, giving us the desire and power to do what pleases Him. Thank God for not only the desire to please Him but also the power to express those desires fully. To follow through on our God given desires is what Jesus calls living life abundantly. It is a life full of satisfaction, purpose and joy. We should not settle for anything less for this is the blessing of God Jabez reached out for and received. Epaphroditus is another who demonstrated a humble serving attitude. His name means lovely and he came to visit Paul in prison representing the believers at Philippi. He almost died in the process but God had mercy on him and spared his life. Paul commends him as a co-worker, true brother and fellow soldier. He took it upon himself to serve his brother and it nearly cost him his life and Paul wanted to commend him for this act of love. Philippians 4.

Desire and power both come from God at work within our human spirits as the Holy Spirit breaks down our natural selfishness and causes us to rather please God and help others. God desires a broken, repentant, dependent and willing spirit. It pleases God when we repent to fight the good fight. It pleases God when we create time and space to listen to Him through His word and pray to Him. It pleases God when we apply His word to our lives and obey it. It pleases God when we forgive as we have been forgiven and love as Christ loves.

In Romans 10: 15-21 Paul is encouraging us to continue calling on the Name of the Lord to continue being saved. Every day is a day to call on the Name of the Lord for salvation from the things of this world. God gives generously to all who call upon Him. Belief in the heart must be confessed with the mouth to be real and authentic. The message is a faith message that requires to be spoken out or confessed. We confess Jesus Christ as Lord and Master the One ruling our lives. If He is ruling then we will have no difficulty in confessing. Messengers who bring good news have beautiful feet because what we believe we will confess. People readily confess their unbelief, which is very sad as it separates from God both here and in eternity if not repented from. Confession connects to God and His eternal glory. The tongue has the power of life and death and those who love it will eat its fruit. Faith is a continuous message of confession and belief from the heart and even if we fall seven times we must rise again and continue the race. We are made right in God's sight from start to finish by faith so we require faith from start to finish. Everybody enduring to the end shall be saved. We must cross the finishing line to finish what God has started in us to get the prize for which God has called us heavenwards in Jesus Christ our Lord. Any other teaching is false and leads to ungodliness. We must beware of false teaching in this area infiltrating the Church and causing believers to compromise. We are called to run a cross country race of faith where we may fall seven times but get up and continue running to finish and cross the line. God has given us the desire and power to run, get up and finish. Grace saves us, makes us righteous and keeps us right to the very end of the race. Now because of His grace we are made righteous and given the confidence we will inherit eternal life. Titus 3: 4-7.

27

NATURAL AND
SUPERNATURAL FIRE

J ohn the Baptist said we would be baptized in the Holy Spirit and
fire. Matthew 3: 11. Tongues and flames of fire fell on the believers
at Pentecost. Acts 2: 3-4. The fire came and rested upon each believer
equipping them to serve God powerfully. This was a glory fire to help
them bring in the harvest from among the nations and the same fire is
about to fall again. It is the fire we see in Exodus 3 where God appeared
to set a bush on fire yet it was not consumed. This fire rests upon us and
does nothing to consume unless we are full of sin. It is a fire resting on
holy ground and we are called to be holy ground. Moses had his own
encounter with the God of fire and we must have ours. He was going
about his business with his sheep like any other day when God broke
in through fire. The fire starts speaking to him from the middle of
the bush because God was in the fire. The fire reveals his purpose and
calling even though Moses did not really want it. He was a reluctant
hero because he didn't want his life interrupted by fire, he didn't want
to return to the land where he was considered to be a murderer. God
was anointing him with fire to fight fire, with supernatural fire to fight

natural fire. Like Moses we will be anointed to do signs, wonders and miracles after our encounter with the God of fire.

Elijah followed Moses with encounters with the God of supernatural fire. 2 Kings 1: 10-14 and chapter 17. Wherever Elijah went, fire followed. The fire of God is revelatory fire. When God turns up in fire people tend to believe and turn back to Him. They are very wise to do so. An evil ruler sends two teams of thugs to arrest Elijah who calls down fire from heaven and they are history. The third captain came with a very different attitude, down on his hands and knees. A God of fire is best approached down on our hands and knees, with the greatest of respect. He has the power of life and death in His fire.

In Exodus 19: 18 and 24: 17 we see God coming down to earth in the form of fire. This will happen again when Jesus returns with the angels in flaming fire to judge all unbelievers. 2 Thessalonians 1: 7. God's supernatural fire is both life giving and life taking and the same is true for natural fire. In Revelation 1: 14 Jesus appears to Apostle John with eyes like flaming fire. Gone is the gentle, harmless little baby in the manger at Bethlehem. Apostle Peter tells us that the present heavens and earth will be judged by fire and destroyed. 2 Peter 3: 7-12. Everything godless will melt away in the flames so that God can create a new heavens and earth filled with His righteousness. The two witnesses in Revelation 11 are two fire filled prophets protected by the fire of God for a season. They will be sent to represent God as His witnesses during the tribulation period and of course it may well be Moses representing the Law and Elijah the prophets. There will be a witness of fire to the nations at the end times and I believe it is soon to begin and we must be ready to participate in it. God describes His angel messengers as flames of fire. Psalm 104: 4 and Hebrews 1: 7. When you have an encounter with an angel expect fire. In 1 Corinthians 3: 10-15, Apostle Paul tells us that on the day of judgement fire will reveal what kind of work and what value of work, each believer has done. This is not judgemental but revelatory fire. This fire will evaluate the quality of our works and service for Christ throughout our lives and it is associated with eternal rewards. Every believer is compared to a builder using materials to build on the one foundation already laid, Jesus Christ our Lord.

Peter, James and John were witnesses to the appearing of Moses and Elijah when they came to visit Jesus and discuss His crucifixion and resurrection on the Mount of Transfiguration. Luke 9: 28-36. Later on, Peter was given permission to mention this incident in 2 Peter 1: 16-18. It is because of this incident that some imagine Moses and Elijah may be the two prophets previously mentioned from Revelation 11 and I think this has some credibility, time will tell. In Luke 16: 19-31, Jesus gives us a story or parable about two men, one rich and one poor. The rich man is unnamed but the beggar is called Lazarus or the one whom God favours. Their lives overlap but are lived out in complete contrast. One is excessively wealthy and the other excessively poor, in fact so poor that he suffered physically and probably died prematurely. This story could be a summary of the state of the world today and the huge poverty gaps between the rich and the poor. Scotland is no different and the popularity and necessity of food banks proves the point. Without them many would starve. Praise God if your church has one as it is a great way to share the love of God in your local community or at your gate.

The rich man could have helped the poor man but he chose not to because he did not regard him as of value or significance. Every time the rich man left his home, he had to pass the poor man begging outside his gates. The poor man was the rich man's opportunity to love and show compassion and kindness but he chose to ignore him. The rich man was no stranger to the law of God and prophets but he chose to ignore them. They pointed him to a responsibility to share with those in need around him, especially the book of Proverbs where he would have noticed that showing kindness to the poor is pleasing to God. Both men eventually die and enter the reality of eternity but two very different realities separated by a great chasm. The rich man is in torment in flames which do not kill him but cause him great mental, spiritual and emotional suffering because his soul and spirit live on eternally. You need to realise that your soul and spirit cannot die, they are eternal because you are made in the image and likeness of the Eternal God. The rich man is fully aware of his past life and very conscious and concerned for his rich brothers and he wants Lazarus to return to earth as an evangelist to warn them to change their attitudes. However, the law and the prophets, which he had rejected are enough for them and God's standard for justice. His request is denied by Abraham the father of all having faith. Faith is required leading to good works to enter the kingdom of God. The rich man had turned his back on Lazarus and God by ignoring his obvious needs and failing to care for him. He is held accountable for his lifestyle of self-indulgence and selfishness. He is held accountable for his lack of faith leading to generosity to others outside his gate. He is left separated from God and His love for all eternity with the possibility that his family may follow.

Jesus is telling us this story to make us aware of our responsibility as regards how we choose to use material wealth and possessions. Lazarus was his human brother so the rich man had a responsibility to help him in every way. He could easily afford to do so after all. God values all men and women made in His image and likeness but we live in a world that is not a level playing field. Faith in God means making every effort to reach out and correct this injustice. We need to value those valued by our heavenly Father and act accordingly for our faith to be real and authentic. The poor are around us everywhere today it is impossible to escape their desperation. Do something to help them by faith and God will reward you because His heart goes out to them. There is a realm of fire for everybody who fails to listen to God's Word and repent from sinful selfishness. We are held accountable by God for the kind of lifestyle we choose to adopt and follow. Be kind to the poor and honour God who loves them and wants to bless them through your kindness. Take some time to talk to poor people and get to know them personally, this means a huge amount to them because often they feel invisible. Buy them some food or a hot drink and tell them you want to pray for them and watch God at work in their lives, there is nothing greater. Do this by faith and God will greatly bless you. Try to develop a relationship with them by taking time to speak to and more importantly listen to them. A listening ear is the most important gift to give, because many may sense nobody values them enough to listen to them. Poor people often feel discouraged because they feel unfairly judged by society especially those considered to be begging on the streets for their well- being which may include a drug addiction as well as food and clothing for their families. Give them the benefit of the doubt and a chance to show you who they really are and what they have the potential to become. Surely this is exactly what Jesus would do for them. Go out into your community gate and do exactly the same. It is time to see a Church without walls and barriers that has the power and desire to make a real difference everywhere throughout the land. Take the hand of Jesus and walk where He walks to experience the power and love of God working through you. This is the supernatural fire of God at work and it is wonderful to behold.

Moses was a man who had experienced the fire of God and it had changed him permanently, he would never be the same again. In Deuteronomy 34, God takes him up Pisgah Peak and shows him the promised land, promised to Abraham, Isaac and Jacob and their descendants but he is not permitted to enter because God was calling him home and he was about to die. Moses has to surrender to the will of God there and can only see the land from a distance but he is about to enter another promised land where he will live with God forever. Moses had to be willing to let go of this life to enter the next because his time had come to an end despite the fact, he was not ill in any way. Deuteronomy 34: 7. There is no record of Moses debating over this with the Lord, he simply surrenders and dies having faithfully finished all God had asked of him. The people take thirty days to mourn for him and celebrate his wonderful life and leadership. Joshua steps forward to take the baton and move the people in a new direction.

The time for Moses to depart had come and the time for Joshua to begin had come. God immediately gives Joshua promises to strengthen and encourage his faith because He wants him to be a strong and courageous leader so perhaps Joshua felt fear and some anxiety taking on this great responsibility from Moses. After all, Moses had been used by God to do signs, wonders and miracles of deliverance for the people of Israel, he was a tough act to follow. God promises to give him success and prosperity in every area of his life and leadership if he studies and meditates on the Torah, the first five books of the Bible. 2 Timothy 3: 14-17. Perhaps you are reading this at a season of change in your own life. God may be asking you to surrender and lay the old down to take up the new. Does He want to give you a new revelation or vision for this new decade? For Joshua this meant thanking God for Moses and the past, then moving on into the present because there was still work to be done to realise the promises of God. We cannot dwell on the things of the past for too long, let them go and move on into all God has prepared and is equipping you to do. Surrender the past as it is dead and cannot be resurrected because the best is yet to come, God has kept the best wine to last. John 2: 1-12. Jesus is about to reveal His glory through you and your faith in Him.

Joshua gives the people three days to prepare to move on into the promises of God. Joshua 1: 10-11. The first challenge they face is the city of Jericho but God had already been there ahead of them to visit a prostitute named Rahab. In Matthew 1: 5 we read that Salmon was the father of Boaz, whose mother was this same Gentile woman Rahab. It's quite possible that Salmon was one of the two Hebrew spies she gave refuge to in the city. Ruth 4: 16-22 tells us she went on to become king David's great, great grandmother. She had been a Gentile woman, formerly a prostitute, who married into the Messianic seed line. Rahab did not allow her past to determine her future. She saw an opportunity to break free from her past and took it eagerly by faith. In her dialogue with the two spies in Joshua 2, it is clear she has heard all about Israel's God Yahweh, and real faith had sprung up in her heart. She had faith for herself and her whole family. She confesses Yahweh as the supreme God of heaven above and earth below. She finds herself in a position to help the spies by giving them safe refuge but in return she wants the guarantee of security for herself and her family. When Jericho eventually falls, she and her family are adopted into the family of God and become a living part of God's purposes for Israel and the Gentile nations. God's grace had opened the way for Rahab to leave her past behind and enter into the circle of God, where He now had her all to Himself. She is a forerunner for all Gentiles placing our faith in God. Like Rahab we are saved by God's grace and taken into a circle surrounded by His love. God now has us all to Himself and can reveal Himself and His plans for our lives to us. All we need do is surrender our plans to His.

By waiting on God, we are opening a door of willingness to explore and discover His plans for us. This can only be a good thing. To wait on God is to have your heart entwined to His until you hear Him speak into your life. Psalm 40: 1-5; Isaiah 40: 28-31. God will always walk through that open door. Revelation 3: 20. This is the way of faith. Faith is the key to opening a door into another reality. It gives us access to the things we long for. Faith proves the unseen, invisible realm. By faith it becomes a reality and a testimony that God speaks and creates the visible from the invisible. Both realities are connected together by faith. It moves us to choose God's way over ours. A faith sacrifice to God is always going to please Him. Enoch was so full of faith that he went straight from this earthly realm to the heavenly without experiencing death, he was simply promoted for pleasing God.

Like Noah, we need to open our hearts to receive revelation and warnings from God about what is coming, even if our faith condemns the world, it must be revealed to save those yet appointed for salvation. We need to obey God's call and receive our inheritance, everything promised, yet to be fulfilled. We are moving forward on a journey of faith with a destination, a city with unshakeable foundations, whose architect and builder is God Himself. We may have to die clinging to our faith but we can still embrace the promises from afar because we live our lives as those belonging to another realm, the heavenly realm. We have a heavenly city ready and prepared for us as our home.

Faith is powerful, inspirational and prophetic. It clothes us with our true identity and promises great reward. It opens a way when there is no way and pulls down the walls and strongholds of God's enemies. It fastens onto God's promises and pulls them into reality. Although weak, our faith imparts power to make us strong. It sparks courage within to become mighty warriors in battle causing enemy armies to flee. The angelic warriors, wheel into battle formation ready to fight alongside us by our faith. Now is the time to step into faith's fullness and see the glory of God revealed to the nations. God is calling us up into a new higher realm of faith to finally access the things we all long for.

28

W'S STORY

My name is W and I am now a believer but it took until I was 74. If only I had believed before I think my life could have been very different but perhaps not, God alone knows. I had quite a happy childhood being the oldest of four and as such I always felt I had to set my younger siblings a good example to follow. My parents were both hard working and very kind to us and the neighbours and the house was full of friendly people most of the time. My mother was a cleaner and my father worked in the insurance business so we always had food on the table and some left over to share with others. My father had fought in the second world war and he had done some boxing in the army which made him a tough man but he was always warm to his family.

When I was in my early twenties, we had a disaster in the family when my younger brother took his own life and I remember it being a really dark and difficult time for all of us because nobody seemed to know why he had done it. It came right out of the blue and shocked the whole community. It made me question God and took me many years to recover from it. I felt really guilty that I didn't notice and perhaps could have helped him. Life went on and I got married and had a son a year later and he proved to be a great comfort to my mother still grieving my younger brother. I worked mainly in retail and my husband was a welder but when he returned from National Service, I could tell he had changed but he wouldn't talk to anybody about it. He started drinking heavily and this put a strain on all of our relationships but most of the time he managed to hold down a steady job so we just got on with things. We managed to get our first house in Inverness but we had a struggle making ends meet and life was quite hard. I worked in the local fish shop in the market and was very happy there although it was freezing cold most of the time to keep the fish fresh.

The years went by and then I got pregnant again and had a little girl. I had to get back to work as soon as possible because we couldn't afford trying to survive on my husband's wages. Sometimes he would come home with nothing because he had been drinking and we had to borrow money from my parents but then my dad took unwell and eventually died from lung cancer. I felt bad for my children because we could never afford holidays and they usually spent their school holidays picking rasps and playing with their friends. I remember going to a local church with my husband and son when he was about three years old. My husband knew the minister who used to have a dram with him. It was harvest thanks-giving day and we sat right at the back. The church was full of fruit and bread and it was all stacked up at the front. My little boy's eyes were nearly popping out of his head, he had never seen so much food and when the minister suddenly appeared, he shouted at the top of his voice, I want an apple from the king! Well, we were mortified and I went bright red with embarrassment but everybody was laughing so that helped. It was the first and last time we ever went to that church. We had neighbours on either side who were very religious people but one beat his wife up regularly and the other used to phone the police whenever my boy played football against the prison wall by the house on a Sunday. They were not exactly a good shop window for Christianity or church so we never bothered with it apart from weddings and funerals.

My son left home for college when he was eighteen and I really missed him but it was the best move for him as he was needing to get away from home and see a different world. His little sister missed him as well and so did the dog. My life took another turn for the worst when my husband was diagnosed with cancer and taken into the local hospice. He managed to give his daughter in marriage just before he died and now, I was on my own. On one occasion my son came home to stay with me for a while and brought his friend round to pray for me because I felt quite unwell and as they prayed, I felt an amazing peace come over me. His friend asked me if I would like to invite Jesus into my life and I did so in He came as I prayed and the peace remained with me. I started to attend a local church where I met an amazing friend who took me along to a local church club, we both really enjoyed. She stayed round the corner so I could visit her easily and the club was also just round the corner. She was a great Christian whom I greatly enjoyed and respected. I consider myself really blessed to have met my Lord at 74. My daughter stayed local and has a lovely little boy whom I love dearly. I just want to say in closing that you do not need to fear the future because God's goodness and love pursue you every day of your life. And afterwards when this life is over, we will return to His glorious presence to be forever with Him. Psalm 23 TPT. W's story is given by permission.

29

DEBORAH, JAEL, BARAK AND GIDEON FAITH AND FIRE

Israel, the people of God are once again under the oppression of their enemies in the promised land, enemies who should not be there but they had made a come- back because they had failed to remove them completely. Deborah was an honourable woman with wisdom, revelation and discernment and she had a prophetic gift where she could hear the word of the Lord. Her husband was Lapidoth, whose name means torch or firebrand so she is married to a light giver. Deborah's name means bee and like a bee she could sting when provoked but she was willing to put her own life at risk for the words she spoke for the good of God's people. Deborah was also a mother in Israel, she was a prophetic, mothering, worshiping warrior, who interceded for her people and heard the word of the Lord to deliver them. We need more Deborah's today who are provoked by the state of the world and hear God's strategies for deliverance. When God wanted to move in a supernatural way, He chose a mother to reveal it to because He had a new revelation for her that would change a nation but she needed others to also play their part in God's story. The prophets cannot do it all on their own, they need the warriors to rise up and follow their insights for victory. In Judges 5: 12 we are told that God told Deborah to waken up to a new revelation because He had something quite unique and special for her to speak. She needed bold and courageous men and women to work with her.

Jael was one of the women Deborah needed and her name means mountain goat. She was surefooted and determined to make a difference and she struck Sisera inside her tent until he was dead. Victory for Israel came from within the tent of a relative of Moses' father-in-law, whose wife remained determined to obey her God. Barak's name means lightning flash and he was a heavenly light giving spiritual and military leadership, a type of Christ. Barak is mentioned alongside Gideon in Hebrews 11: 32 in the Faith Hall of Fame. He had responded to Deborah's word to call out ten thousand warriors to fight Sisera, commander of king Jabin's Canaanite army oppressing Israel. Deborah had prophesied that God would give Barak victory if he was willing to engage him in battle on a plain, which sounds crazy because Sisera had nine hundred iron chariots and this kind of battle terrain would suit him perfectly. But God had a plan and just before the battle began a storm arose and Sisera's chariots became useless, he was now at the mercy of Barak and his warriors who completely routed him. Deborah had also prophesied that a woman would kill Sisera not Barak as he had insisted, she accompany them to the battle field. Barak's faith is activated when Deborah tells him the Lord has gone ahead of him and the victory is secured when Sisera escapes to Jael's tent where she kills him as he lies asleep and exhausted. She is remembered as most blessed among women who live in tents for her faithfulness and courage. Judges 5: 24-27. Ordinary women of God living in their homes are capable of extra-ordinary feats of faith and how we thank God for them. God needed a Deborah, Deborah needed a Barak and Barak needed a Jael for the final victory to emerge, where the people of God were liberated and set free to worship Yahweh once again. All three had paved the faith way for Gideon to emerge some forty years later.

God had a sense of humour when He called Gideon, whose name means one who cuts to pieces. Just before the angel appeared to Gideon, God had sent another prophet to tell the people they had been suffering due to their disobedience and idolatry. Gideon, son of Joash of the tribe of Abiezer had an encounter with an angel while hiding from the oppressive Midianites in a winepress, he was behaving far from a mighty warrior but God had seen something in him nobody else had. Mighty warrior, God is with you, must have seemed ironic to Gideon hiding away in his basement for fear of his enemies. God was declaring his true identity and destiny over him even though he felt far removed from it. He treats us in exactly the same way. Gideon had issues with God! He doesn't feel like a mighty warrior and he doesn't believe God is with him or Israel. We cannot blame him for feeling this way because he was disappointed and felt abandoned by God. Despite this he wanted to see God's miracles again but he needed convincing God was willing and up for the fight. How many of us feel just like Gideon right now? Gideon felt overwhelmed by the state of the nation but God recruits him despite his feelings of disappointment, abandonment and doubt. Gideon was honest before God, he didn't hold anything back, even though at the time he didn't actually know this was an angel messenger speaking to him.

God now tells Gideon what He told Moses and Joshua that I will be with you Gideon! This is God's way of telling him he cannot fail as all the resources of heaven are now available to him. Gideon is now embarking on a faith journey with God where he is beginning to believe more and perhaps take the action his faith requires. God is building him up in his faith for all that lies ahead and He is very patient with him. God and Gideon are now sharing the same dream and God is equipping Gideon to fulfil it. Proverbs 13: 12. God is taking Gideon out of that low place in the winepress and building up his faith and confidence in Him. He is a mighty hero hiding at the bottom of a winepress but now God is with him and ready to send him to realise his dream, to set Israel free from their enemies. Just how many of God's mighty heroes are hiding at the bottom of the winepress? Arise, like Gideon and emerge into the sunlight of God's glory for your life. God is telling us that He knows we feel weak and inferior but He wants what we have no matter what and He will do the rest. Gideon gives God the little he has and trusts God for the rest. He is like the little boy giving Jesus five of one and two of the other to feed five thousand people but God takes it and does it anyway! Gideon makes a meal for this angel, who then consumes it by fire and disappears and he then realises he was speaking to an angel from God. He rightly panics but God reassures him, he is not going to die! He marks the spot of the encounter by building an altar to Yahweh Shalom the Lord is peace. Gideon was convinced by the God of fire and now he is more ready to serve Him. But there was a family problem involving idolatry and God tells Gideon to go and fix it. Gideon now has the faith to do so even though it could have cost him his life. He destroys the altar to Baal and replaces it with an altar to Yahweh and sacrifices his father's seven-year- old bull upon it. God is telling Gideon to honour Him before his family and trust Him for the consequences. Gideon's faith requires courage and boldness, this is a sign from God of what's to come. The men from the town want to kill him but his father steps in to protect and deliver him. He is a picture of the Father sending His Son from heaven to deal with sin and Satan and set the people free.

Gideon's faith is touched again and he raises an army of 32,000 men to fight a Midianite army of 135,000 men. But once again Gideon needs God to reassure him that He will be faithful to His promises. He is not quite ready for the big fight and God is patient with him. He asks for three more signs including the interpretation of a divine dream before he feels ready. Judges 6: 33-40 and 7: 12-16. Now he feels ready but God decides to whittle his army down first to 10,000 then to 300 men. God wants Israel to be in no doubt that it will be His supernatural power giving the victory rather than fighting soldiers. The three hundred men left with Gideon must have shared his faith or they would never have agreed to accompany him into battle because God's strategy seemed strange. They were to surround the enemy camp and blow shofar horns and break fire-filled clay pots before shouting for the Lord and for Gideon! This is an example of Proverbs 1: 2-5. TPT. God has given Gideon a strategy for leadership which is a brilliant tree of life for Israel.

Gideon proves it is never wrong to ask God for signs you are moving in the right direction. He went on to rule Israel for forty years but during that time he made mistakes. He made an idol from gold which caused people to stumble and he slept with a concubine whose son murdered seventy of his children from his other wives. Despite this, Gideon rises up into the Hall of Faith Fame in Hebrews 11: 32-35. His life shows us how patient God is as He develops our faith and brings us to a place where He can secure our destiny plans. Gideon was an ordinary man doubting God and himself, whom God transformed to rescue a nation and lead them for forty years. You and I are just like him and we have the same God. Mighty hero, the Lord is with you.

Like Gideon many of us have probably had encounters with angels that we are not aware of sent by God to help us out in a time of need. You may feel deep down in the winepress of fear, disappointment and low self-esteem but remember so was Gideon and the Lord had not abandoned him. Tell Him how you feel because He knows anyway and rest assured, He loves you and will work with anything you can give to Him even weakness, fear and doubt. God is patient with us giving us all the time we need to grow in faith and trust Him more and more. Gideon is a great example of a man on a journey of faith with a destiny and a dream from God. God shows real commitment to Gideon because he is His son and He wants him to succeed. Gideon had an inheritance that God wanted to give him and He waited patiently until he was ready to receive it and we are no different. Put your hands afresh into God's today and give Him all you have and He will do the rest. Gideon shows us that when we make mistakes and repent, we can still end up in the Hall of Faith in Heaven. He had flaws just like the rest of us but God used him anyway because he was obedient and did exactly what God was asking him to do and that took real solid faith. We need to go and do the same because faith requires actions to become kingdom material. It is like clay in the hands of the Potter that He takes and moulds into something beautiful for His glory. Mighty hero, the Lord is with you.

There is a faith journey through the psalms, which the Holy Spirit has left for us all to make. It is a journey through ten very special psalms called the Numbers psalms from psalm 91 to psalm 100. Psalm 91 begins the first step of the journey and it describes our relationship with God and His marvellous promises. God is our great confidence, rescuing us from every trap of the enemy. He is the Father with massive arms wrapped around His children to protect them. The demonic realms are unable to break through God's covering as His angel armies defend us from harm. We are promised the inheritance of God's full salvation. With every journey there is a first step and this first step makes the rest of the journey possible.

In Psalm 92 we have a prophetic praise song for the day of worship on the Sabbath. Jewish tradition holds that Adam composed this psalm on the first Sabbath of creation. It was sung by the Levites on the Sabbath in the Temple. The psalm celebrates depths of purpose and meaning behind everything God does. It celebrates the amazing mysteries of God to be found within every one of His miracles. It speaks about the anointing of the Holy Spirit coming to make us strong and mighty as He empowers with fresh daily oil. Even in older age we are promised fruitfulness, flourishing, health and vitality.

Psalm 93 is the Friday psalm. The Jewish Talmud indicates this psalm was sung by the Levites in the Temple on a Friday. It declares God's sovereign rule over everything because He has reigned as King over everything since time began. God rules from an eternal realm where His children will join Him as it is kept in heaven for us until we die. Though chaos may challenge God and His people, it shall not overcome because it is stilled under God's voice as Jesus, when He spoke to the wind and waves on Lake Galilee. God's house are His people made holy by the blood of Jesus, the Lamb of God.

Psalm 94 was sung by the Levites on the fourth day of the week or a Wednesday in the Temple. It sings about God's right to take vengeance against His enemies and everything evil. It looks forward to judgement day when the Judge of all the earth will do right and God's people will be rewarded for their faithfulness. Nations and individuals will stand before God's judgement throne to be examined by Yah, the God of power. Justice will prevail as God punishes the wicked and blesses the righteous.

Psalm 95 declares the time to praise the Lord with a new song because He is the God who saves us. Our shouts of joyful praise make

God great and exalt Him over all other gods. We must kneel in reverence before Him and listen to His voice. We are to follow His ways and keep His words. We must enter into God's resting place by coming to Jesus for rest and leaving our cares and burdens with Him. Matthew 11: 28-30.

Psalm 96 celebrates the King of the world. He is the saving King who saves every day and is most worthy of praise. He made the heavens and the nations to glorify His Name. We are invited into His courts to worship in reverence and awe. The nations need to know that Lord Yahweh reigns because He is coming to judge the world. Even His creation will welcome this with shouts of praise and glory.

In psalm 97, God is returning with fire. The fire spreads ahead to judge His enemies and the whole world is under the spotlight of His lightning flashes. Every knee bows down before Him because He is supreme and the exalted One protecting the lives of His godly people, rejoicing in Him.

Psalm 98 is a new song to Yahweh for His wonderful deeds. Victory and saving power belong to Him. He is the faithful One of Israel, His covenant people. Everything with breath praises Him in one joyful symphony as we all stand before Him.

Psalm 99 pictures Yahweh seated on His throne between the cherubim and it reminds us of the vision of Isaiah in Isaiah 6. We are to exalt the Lord our God and bow low before Him for He alone is holy. Moses, Aaron and Samuel are three of His heroes interceding before the throne for Israel.

Psalm 100 finishes the journey and how appropriate it is as God opens the door of heaven and invites us in to worship Him with great joy. We must come respecting His protocol by entering His gates with thanksgiving and His courts with praise. It is a great home coming psalm for every believer. We are coming home to the One who has been waiting for us to welcome us in. His love for us is faithful and endures forever. We are coming into the atmosphere of heaven to be forever with Him. Here we see the Father with arms outstretched welcoming us home to our forever home. Ten psalms leading us step by step on a journey of faith into the presence of God and home to be with the Father.

30

THE COMING FIRE

There is Pentecostal fire described in Joel and Acts that will help us to understand the fire that is coming. In Joel, four kinds of locust are mentioned and each has one thing in common, they eat the crops and strip the land bare leaving behind economic devastation in Israel. This vast army may be enemy nations attacking Israel causing terrible destruction. God calls His people to a season of prayer with fasting to break this oppression because the Day of the Lord's return is near, Joel 1: 14. Later on in the chapter we read about possible results of climate change in Israel as wild fires burn out of control in the promised land. Joel 1: 19-20. Joel may be looking into the future and seeing the times of Jacob's Trouble or what others call the Great Tribulation. Jesus spoke about this in Matthew 24. It is interesting that Joel also sees the sudden arrival of the Lord's angel armies with Jesus Himself at the head of the army, Joel 2: 1-11.

This mighty army is described as being like the roar of a fire sweeping across a field of stubble. Fire burns in front and flames follow after them. Joel 2: 12 is the call to repentance now, while there is still time. God is calling for repentant hearts alongside fasting, weeping and mourning. He is calling His people together to the Temple to pray for merciful intervention. Joel 2: 12-17. It seems that the people respond and here we have the turning point in the prophecy, Joel 2: 18. God delivers His people by driving out the foreign armies and begins to make the land fruitful again. A miracle of deliverance and provision occurs followed by a spiritual outpouring on all God's people. Joel 2: 31 indicates these events will occur before the great and glorious day of the Lord's return to Israel. Two events seem to be occurring simultaneously, a restoration of Israel materially and spiritually and a judgement on the foreign nations harming and scattering the people and dividing up the land. Joel 3: 1-3.

God regathers His scattered people and calls for a time of war where He fights with His warriors both for His people and His land. Joel 3: 9-13. The lord's voice will roar from Zion and thunder from Jerusalem and the heavens and earth will shake. At this time foreign armies will never again conquer Israel or Jerusalem because the Lord Himself will make His home among them there. Joel 3: 20-21. The fire that is coming is going to fall on the Jewish people, causing them to repent and turn back to God and His Messiah. God is about to intervene and save them from both physical and spiritual enemies.

These are the very Scriptures Peter uses in his speech in Acts 2 on the Day of Pentecost, when the Holy Spirit falls on the believers in flames of fire. Acts 2: 1-4. The fire causes Peter to boldly proclaim the Good News and three thousand converts are added to the church in one day. Here we see the same man having denied His Lord in fear weeks before now proclaiming Him in bold power after an encounter with the fire of the Holy Spirit. The new converts were people from Mesapotamia, Asia, Libya, Egypt and many other nations as well as local Jewish people. Many would now return to their own nations as baptised believers. The fire that rested on Peter at Pentecost gave him tremendous boldness and clarity of mind to understand and communicate the truth in God's Word as revealed through the life of Jesus the Living Word. But not only that, people began to be supernaturally healed beginning with a crippled beggar outside the Temple. This sign and wonder resulted in another two thousand people becoming believers. Acts 4: 4. It was after this miracle that persecution broke out against the believers in Jerusalem. The fire saves, heals and then provokes opposition and persecution. But then the fire causes the believers to pray for courage in the face of opposition and persecution. In Acts 4: 31 we read that after prayer their meeting place shook and once again, they were all filled with the Holy Spirit and fire, so they could continue preaching boldly and fearlessly. God's answer to opposition is more fire!

God's fire releases sign's and wonders among the people and brings the believers together in unity of mind and purpose. Acts 4: 31-37. New believing communities are formed which reflect the Kingdom of God. Despite growing opposition every day in the Temple and from house to house, the believers continue to teach and preach that Jesus is the Messiah. The fire causes God's message to continue to spread and eventually it reaches the Gentiles or non-Jews as Philip preaches in Samaria and Peter in Caesarea. Acts 8: 4-40 and Acts 10: 1-48. This is exactly what Jesus spoke about in Acts 1: 8 and here it's happening. The Jewish believers are initially amazed that the Holy Spirit is being received by Gentiles, as they hear them speaking in tongues and prophesying. Acts 10: 44-48. The fire leaps across religious and cultural differences bringing everyone with faith into an encounter with God. It is unstoppable, unquenchable and uncontrollable. It is the fire of God determined to burn wherever He sends it.

In Acts 13: 1-3 we learn that the fire is kindled through worship, prayer and fasting. In this environment the Holy Spirit speaks and separates Barnabas and Saul to continue carrying the fire outside of Antioch. God then uses the Apostles and others to plant and establish new believing communities wherever they go and the gospel begins to transform pagan areas such as Corinth, Ephesus and the Greek islands. The fire causes riots in pagan cities where idolatrous industries are affected by it. Paul is so filled with fire that he writes two thirds of the New Testament moved by its power. He wants to hand the fire over to us, so that we will continue to spread it until Christ returns. So how are we doing? What are we doing with God's fire? In 1 Thessalonians 5: 19-20 we are told never to restrain or put out the fire of the Holy Spirit and never scorn the prophetic. We need prophets and prophecy to keep the fire burning in our hearts. 1 Corinthians 12-14. Prophecy is given to strengthen the entire church but also to convict unbelievers and bring them to faith in God. We need prophets released in the church and on the streets because God places great value on both. 1 Corinthians 14: 1. The fire of the Holy Spirit will return to our churches when we honour the prophetic, supernatural, giftings of God and release one another into them. We need to ask God for forgiveness for the way we have scorned the prophetic and dampened the fire of God.

God is going to send prophetic waves of power into Israel and throughout the nations to bring in His final End Times harvest from among the nations. Will we commit ourselves to become a meaningful part of this prophetic move of God and participate in it? The fire is coming. Don't be a spectator be a participant. A river of fire is coming from the throne to cover the nations and God wants us to embrace and become a living part of it. The reason God told me to write this book was to help prepare His people to run with fire. Will you be one who will run with God's fire for the fire is coming?

— 31 —

D'S STORY

H i I am D and I grew up in a so- called Christian home but there was a lot of physical abuse from my father. My mother had struggles with alcohol as well. Most Sundays I was taken to church but I never had a personal relationship with Christ. My dad would also regularly cheat on my mum. At the age of twelve, I was taken out of my home for my own safety and put into a children's unit. I spent the next four years in three different children's units and they were full of misery and deeply hurting children. I felt little hope and no purpose in the homes. I stopped going to school when I was thirteen. During this time, I had weekly contact with my mum and loved her visits. I had no contact with my dad and didn't see him for another fifteen years. I really did love my mum she had a real heart for people. When I was sixteen my mum died really suddenly and it completely destroyed me. I ended up in hospital after a suicide attempt, which was really a cry for help!

This led to me spending the next six years of my life in a psychiatric hospital in social isolation. To cope I ate constantly and ended up weighing forty- three stone. The hospital was a horrible place and I spent most of my time alone apart from some time in the dorms with the drug addicts. A lot of people were self- harming. My friend had originally been sent to a psychiatric hospital for murder but appeared at my general ward hoping for release but he died of a heart attack very suddenly. In the last few months of my stay a young man in the dorm tried to hang himself. I had become institutionalised and the thought of leaving hospital terrified me as I was suffering from severe anxiety and depression and felt I had no hope at all. Eventually a care package was agreed for me and I left the hospital to get my own flat with twenty-four- hour care in the community.

I could hardly do anything because of my weight and size as over eating had become my way of self-harming. One day I began to experience pain in my head and eyes and after contacting the hospital was diagnosed with meningitis. I was absolutely terrified, crying and shaking as I knew this could be a death sentence. That day a Christian woman had been at my house and spoke to me about Christ but I was very angry and questioned how God could allow so much pain and suffering. As I was facing death, I felt I couldn't pretend anymore and I knew there was a Hades and a God. I felt that if I died, I was going to Hades so I cried out to God and asked Him to save me that night and promised Him that if He did, I would give Him my all. I suddenly felt great peace come all over me and two days later I was out of hospital all clear of meningitis. I now felt very different as something had changed, I had changed. I had experienced God's forgiveness and merciful healing and within a few years I had lost twenty- three stone and learned to drive. I started to leave the house more and got a dog for more exercise. I began to attend church again to understand what I had been saved from and I began to realise that God was my loving heavenly Father. One day at church I asked God for three things. That I would lose more weight, get closer to God and His people and meet a Christian wife. They all seemed unlikely at the time but all three answers came quite quickly.

I had changed in many ways but I still struggled to forgive my dad. I was carrying pain and hate and could not let it go so I started praying for my dad. One day I felt God leading me to a certain church so I went along and the message was about forgiveness. After the service my dad suddenly appeared and shook my hand, I was in total shock. I didn't know what to say but I felt no anger or hate. This was the first time my dad had attended this church and the first time he had attended any church for three years. God was really speaking to me so I had to deal with it. I began meeting my dad regularly and he paid for me to receive private surgery to lose more weight. We travelled there together for the surgery and this helped to bridge the gap he had left in my life years before. God was really helping me with the forgiveness and I believe it all began when I started to pray for my dad, He brought us together again.

I began attending another church where I met my amazing wife. She is a wonderful woman who has been through intense pain and suffering. She is full of hope and love. My journey of faith continues and I have served God through by reaching out to the homeless and vulnerable. I want to praise God for His continuing goodness to me and my wife. To God be the glory for the things He has done. There is much more to look forward to, now that I am filled with love, joy and peace. I have a purpose and new life in Christ. What God has done for me, He can also do for you if you invite Him into your life and give Him a chance to change things for the better. He will never leave you or forsake you. Bless you, D.

CONCLUSION

THE VISION

There was once a man who was exiled to the island of Patmos for preaching the Word of God and for his testimony about Jesus. It was the Lord's Day and he was worshiping in the Spirit when suddenly he heard a loud voice behind him like a trumpet blast. The voice said, write in a book everything you see and send it to the seven churches in the cities of Ephesus, Smyrna, Pergamum, Thyatira, Sardis, Philadelphia and Laodicea. When he turned to see who was speaking to him, he saw seven golden lampstands and standing in the middle was one like the Son of Man. He was wearing a long robe with a golden sash across His chest. His head and hair were white like wool, as white as snow. His eyes were like blazing fire. His feet were like polished bronze refined in a furnace and His voice thundered like mighty ocean waves. He held seven stars in His right hand and a sharp, two- edged sword came from His mouth. His face was like the sun in all its brilliance. When the man saw Him, he fell at His feet as if he were dead. But He laid His right hand on him and said, don't be afraid, I am the First and the Last. I am the Living One. I died, but look I am alive forever! And I hold the keys of death and the grave.

The man who had the vision was John and his vision is about to be fulfilled.

Luke 12: 49. Jesus came to set the world on fire. What did He mean? In Psalm 69: 9 we read my love for You has my heart on fire. TPT. This is a powerful Messianic psalm frequently quoted in the

New Testament alongside Psalm 22 predicting the crucifixion and resurrection of the Messiah. Jesus went through a terrible baptism of suffering out of His passionate love for us. He wants us to love as passionately as He does. Fire refines and purifies bringing forth new life and new birth. Titus 3: 4-8 speaks about this in more detail. The passionate love of God can become a fire burning in our hearts if we hunger for it. The fire is coming!

Printed in the United States
by Baker & Taylor Publisher Services